P9-CPY-825

The Internet *and the* LAW

What Educators Need to Know

KATHLEEN CONN

Association for Supervision and Curriculum Development
Alexandria, Virginia USA

Association for Supervision and Curriculum Development1703 N. Beauregard St. • Alexandria, VA 22311-1714 USA
Telephone: 800-933-2723 or 703-578-9600 • Fax: 703-575-5400
Web site: http://www.ascd.org • E-mail: member@ascd.org

All Web links in this book are correct as of the publication date below but may have become inactive or otherwise modified since that time. If you notice a deactivated or changed link, please e-mail books@ascd.org with the words "Link Update" in the subject line. In your message, please specify the Web link, the book title, and the page number on which the link appears.

Printed in the United States of America.

ASCD Product No. 102119
ASCD member price: $16.95   nonmember price: $20.95
s8/2002

Library of Congress Cataloging-in-Publication Data
Conn, Kathleen, 1942-
  The Internet and the law : what educators need to know / Kathleen Conn.
     p. cm.
  ISBN 0-87120-677-3 (alk. paper)
  1. Internet—Law and legislation—United States. 2. School administrators—United States—Handbooks, manuals, etc. 3. Educators—United States—Handbooks, manuals, etc. 4. Teachers—United States—Handbooks, manuals, etc. I. Title.
  KF390.5.C6 C6573 2002
  343.7309'944'02437—dc21
                                         2002008420

08 07 06 05 04 03 02   10 9 8 7 6 5 4 3 2 1

The Internet and the Law:
What Educators Need To Know

1722

Acknowledgments

THIS BOOK HAS BEEN—AND MUST CONTINUE TO BE—A WORK IN progress, because the Internet is continuously changing and so, hopefully, is its role in public education. For his patient understanding of this reality and his steadfast encouragement and support of all my endeavors in education and law, I dedicate this book to my husband, Coulson A. Conn.

I would like to thank Bruce Monroe, patent attorney and Adjunct Professor of Law at Widener University School of Law, for carefully reviewing the "black letter law" and inferences from case law in the manuscript. Bruce has an extraordinary intelligence, and I am privileged to call him a friend. Any errors that persist are solely the responsibility of the author.

I also want to express my special appreciation to several colleagues and friends, most of whom are unaware that I was writing this book, but who contributed in subtle ways to its successful completion. Thank you to

- Toni, Becky, "the two Sues," Deb, and Brenda, for keeping me sane in the crazy world of public education;
- The wonderful teachers in the West Chester Area School District, for making me proud of public education; and
- Perry Zirkel, for the simple kindness of personally responding to an e-mail inquiry several years ago, and for giving me a start in education law.

I also would like to acknowledge the many professors at Widener University School of Law, Delaware Campus, who contributed to my understanding of the law. I am proud to be an alumna.

A special thank you to Stephanie Selice, my acquisitions editor at ASCD.

Finally, I cannot forget my children. Their contribution was to endure a mom who never left school. I thank them for being proud of me.

Foreword

"What is the smart thing to do?"

"What kinds of policies and procedures do we need?"

"How has the Internet changed the rules?"

Under the best of circumstances, public school leaders encounter many situations and decisions that require a solid grounding in court decisions and legal issues. Smart districts adopt guidelines and procedures to reduce risk and standardize legal responses. But, no matter how hard they might try to create documents to govern every foreseeable incident or challenge, real problems will still require the application of good sense and judgment.

Here is where *The Internet and the Law: What Educators Need to Know* proves itself a major asset to any school, school district, or school leader. It offers many suggestions for new guidelines, procedures, and documents, but it also defines a range of choices within each major legal category, leaving considerable room for common sense and good judgment.

When it comes to the Internet, public school leaders face a combination of urgency and uncertainty because neither legislators nor the courts have yet provided clear answers to many of the problems that are emerging. Without a thick body of case law and precedents to define what is legal and what is not, the best school leaders can do is make reasonable projections from past decisions and analogous situations.

Making reasonable projections is the skill that sets Conn's work apart, as she does a thorough and comprehensive job of outlining the key issues, identifying the main risks, and proposing a full set of policies and procedures to protect district interests.

The worst thing that a public school district can do, of course, is to wait until trouble happens to ask the questions Conn addresses in her book. The wise course is to think the unthinkable before it happens so preventive steps can be taken and adequate notice can be given to all parties in advance. Conn deftly leads us through this thought process and offers a wide-ranging array of policy and action steps to take before the horses escape the corral.

Well-meaning leaders may differ as to the policies they may adopt that govern such issues as e-mail use by students. Some might take more risks than others in order to enrich program and learning possibilities, but Conn's book will prove useful in defining the risks and suggesting program strategies to minimize them. Her tone and her perspective are calm, dispassionate, and scholarly, even while her language is direct and easy to interpret.

At times, the safest legal strategy—centralizing many network functions and decisions, for example—is not always the wisest course from an educational perspective, but Conn does not prescribe or preach. She describes the options, outlines the implications, offers advice, but still leaves room for local choice. After reading her book and adjusting policies, a district can feel secure in the knowledge that most important issues have been carefully considered and addressed.

Jamie McKenzie
Editor
From Now On:
The Educational Technology Journal

Introduction

SURVEYS BY THE NATIONAL CENTER FOR EDUCATION STATISTICS indicate that 98 percent of U.S. public schools have Internet and World Wide Web access, up from about 35 percent just 10 years ago. More than 75 percent of all schools have Internet access in classrooms where direct instruction takes place. Nearly 38.5 million school-aged children will be online by 2002, according to Cisco Systems Inc. estimates. Clearly, the Internet has become a major part of schools and students' lives in a relatively short time.

What Is the Internet?

The technology gurus who "invented" the Internet designed it to be a decentralized repository for defense-related secrets during wartime. Spurred by the success of the Soviet Union's Sputnik spacecraft, President Dwight Eisenhower created in 1957 the Advanced Research Projects Agency (ARPA). During the 1960s and 1970s, graduate students and professors at the University of California, Los Angeles (UCLA) and Stanford University worked together with colleagues from universities from the East Coast and abroad in developing ARPANET, a network of computers designed to transmit information by "packet switching." In peacetime, the Internet became a common everyday tool for locating, conveying, and expressing information and ideas. It links computers and computer networks around the world, transmitting text, graphics, video, animation, or sounds rapidly to hundreds of millions of users in nearly 200 countries. The World Wide Web, on the other hand, is a subsection of the Internet that consists of documents residing on computers around the world. These documents are formatted in a language called hypertext markup language (HTML), which facilitates finding information and moving between resources.

Creating Web pages is easy to do thanks to inexpensive and readily available software packages. Part of the software then connects the Web pages to the Internet with certain computer protocols; another part of the software makes the pages available to all Internet users worldwide. In fact, with current technology, Web page creators cannot specify where geographically their communications will go. Web pages literally reach out to the world.

How Does the Internet Work?

Internet transmission occurs by breaking information into fragments, or *packets*, with Internet protocol (IP) addresses. The packets of information then upload to the set of interconnected computers on the Internet. *Router* computers send them separately to their destinations, with each packet traveling along the least crowded pathway, and other computers then reassemble the messages at the receiving end. Only the would-be recipients of the Web pages can block or filter their content.

On the other hand, if an Internet user wants to locate information that someone else has posted on the Web, the human searcher uses a *search engine*, an Internet tool that identifies information by its Uniform Resource Locator (URL). The URL is a visible identification tag or address that allows a search engine to find the specific Internet posting. Web pages also have hidden identification tags, called *metatags*, which allow search engines to find and display them. Metatags can specify keywords, document authors, or certain HTML language. Sometimes, unscrupulous Web page creators label their pages with metatags designed to attract searchers who do not really want their information. Some pornography Web sites use familiar and nonpornographic metatags to entice search engines into locating their sites. People who are inexperienced in formulating Internet searches often "hit on," or encounter, inappropriate Web sites because of such metatags.

What Is the Internet Good For?

Teachers can use the Internet in school to download exemplary lesson plans, participate in collaborative professional development initiatives, and even earn graduate credits online. Students can participate in live interactive *Web chats* with scientists, take virtual field trips, contribute data to worldwide weather research projects, explore remote corners of the globe, and dive under the ocean with researchers and adventurers. But teachers can also use the Internet as a technological babysitter, as a vehicle for venting gripes and frustrations to a wide audience, or even to shop for bargains during school time. In addition, students can download research papers, homework, and the latest gossip about schoolmates posted on unofficial school-oriented Web sites. Students can also find information about how to ensure that their "sucks sites" (sites designed to insult or embarrass people) are legal; that is, that the sites' content does not violate either antidefamation statutes or copyright laws. The Internet is a mixed blessing, and nowhere are its attributes met with more mixed reactions than in the public school setting.

The Problem with the Internet in Schools

Because the penetration of the Internet into the public school setting is such a relatively recent phenomenon, educators and administrators are often unprepared to keep up or even to effectively deal with their students' online skills and creativity. School district responses to teachers' and students' Internet use and misuse contain legal ramifications. Moreover, administrators and teachers may not recognize as problematic privacy and other First Amendment issues in the school Internet context. The Internet can also facilitate harassment that may go undetected by administrators or teachers.

What This Book Is About

This book aims to address the needs of administrators and educators for information about the legal aspects of the Internet in K–12 public schools, presented in nonlegal, nontechnical language. Such a book may appear simultaneously presumptuous and futile. The Internet is changing rapidly. Conservative estimates of the rate of growth of the World Wide Web indicate that two million new pages appear each day, and that a Web page's average life is 75 days. Legislatures at both the state and federal level are scrambling to pass laws to regulate Internet commerce and communication. Similarly, courts all over the country are hearing and deciding the merits of lawsuits relating to Internet access and use in schools and school libraries. How can one book purport to represent "the law" when the law in this area is unsettled?

Paradoxically, the change and uncertainty attendant on the vagaries of the Internet and its expansion in public schools, combined with the largely unsettled state of the law, dictate the need for information in a permanent form. Whatever the specific content of Web pages, definite standards developed with regard to what is developmentally and educationally appropriate for children will be used to judge their merit. Whatever the specific facts of a given Internet-related lawsuit, the court will apply tested and accepted legal precepts and precedents to arrive at a decision. This book aims to communicate those general legal principles and apply them to several broad areas of school Internet concerns.

Simply put, the chapters are designed, first, to point out the major Internet-related legal issues, which administrators and educators must recognize and to which they must react. Second, each chapter offers recommendations based on general legal principles that should govern administrators' and educators' responses to school Internet issues. Where the law is currently uncertain, this is noted. Finally, annotated references are supplied at the end of each chapter for anyone who needs more extensive or specific information. At the end of the book, a resources appendix also lists general sources of information about legal developments in the Internet context and in education law generally.

1

The Foundations of School Internet Law

THREE SEMINAL U.S. SUPREME COURT DECISIONS FORM THE foundation of school Internet law. Together, they lay out the guiding principles under which courts analyze school district, administrator, and teacher responses to public school Internet-based controversies. The decisions themselves are not current, but they continue to be timely. Rare is the court decision dealing with schools that does not reference one or more of these three decisions. Understanding the rationale of these three decisions is the beginning of understanding the law with respect to the Internet in public schools.

Decision 1: Expressive Conduct and Its Bounds

The first foundational decision, *Tinker v. Des Moines Independent Community School District*, 393 U.S. 503 (1969), occurred in the context of the Vietnam Conflict. A group of adults and students in Des Moines decided to protest the American involvement in the war by fasting and wearing black armbands. When the principals of the Des Moines secondary schools learned of the plan, they adopted a policy to suspend students who wore armbands to school and refused to remove them. With knowledge of the policy, teenagers John Tinker, his sister Mary Beth, and their friend Christopher Eckhardt still wore the black armbands to school and refused to remove them; they received suspensions. The students, through their parents, filed suit in court. The controversy went all the way to the U.S. Supreme Court, where Justice Abe Fortas noted that the wearing of armbands was akin to "pure speech." Writing for the majority, he articulated the often-quoted phrase, "It can hardly be argued that either students or teachers shed their constitutional rights to freedom of speech or expression at the schoolhouse gate."

The court pointed out that school officials, who were fueled only by an undifferentiated fear of possible school disturbance, sought to punish the students for their "expressive conduct." Such generalized desire to avoid unpleasantness is not enough, the court said, to justify suppressing student expression. When are school authorities justified in suppressing student speech or expressive conduct? The test, which has become known as the *Tinker* test, is whether school authorities have strong reasons to anticipate that the speech or expression would "substantially interfere with the work of the school or impinge upon the rights of other students."

The court also noted that school authorities banned only the black anti-Vietnam War armbands; they did not ban the wearing of any and all political symbols. The prohibition of only one point of view, the court said, without evidence of material and substantial interference with schoolwork or discipline, is unconstitutional. However, student expression that "materially disrupts classwork or involves substantial disorder or invasion of the rights of others" is not constitutionally protected.

Courts at all levels and jurisdictions reiterate the *Tinker* standard of "material and substantial disruption" for judging the constitutional protection available for students' in-school expression. Moreover, courts apply the same *Tinker* standard to student speech or expression that originates outside of school but includes effects within the school.

Decision 2: Sexy Speech Not Passing Muster

Bethel School District No. 403 v. Fraser, 478 U.S. 675 (1986), is the second court decision presaging judicial reasoning in the school-related Internet context. Matthew Fraser, a high school student with sex instead of common sense on his mind, delivered a speech at a school assembly nominating his friend for student council. While hardly anyone knows or even cares how Matthew's friend fared in the election, everyone involved in school law knows what happened to Matthew; the sexually suggestive metaphors laced throughout his speech prompted school officials to suspend him. The court upheld the school district's actions, stating, "the constitutional rights of students in public schools are not automatically coextensive with the rights of adults in other settings." In other words, although Matthew's remarks were not sufficiently graphic to bring down the law on an adult outside of the school setting, they were lewd and vulgar and, therefore, unacceptable in the school setting. The mission of public schools, the Supreme Court said, is to inculcate the fundamental values of civility; the Constitution does not compel school officials to surrender control to students.

Decision 3: The Pen Not So Mighty as the School

The third foundational decision for courts' more recent Internet deliberations is *Hazelwood School District v. Kuhlmeier*, 484 U.S. 260 (1988), a decision prompted by articles written by students for their school newspaper.

Students at Hazelwood East High School in St. Louis, Missouri, were irritated when their principal decided to withhold two student-written articles about teen pregnancy and divorce from the school newspaper. They and their parents filed suit to force publication of the articles and affirm the freedom of the school press. Instead, the Supreme Court affirmed the right of school authorities to censor student expression as long as the censorship decisions are based on legitimate pedagogical concerns.

Departing from and expanding the bases of the decisions in *Tinker* and *Fraser*, the Supreme Court declared that public schools are not open forums for all kinds of speech. Schools, they said, may have to tolerate personal student expression of which school authorities disapprove *under some circumstances*, but they do not have to affirmatively promote all student speech. If people outside the school would view the students' newspaper as bearing the "*imprimatur*" of the school, the court declared, school authorities may exercise broad discretion to ensure that such expression comports with educational objectives.

The Legal Standard of Conduct

To a nonlawyer, as well as to many lawyers, the Supreme Court's pronouncements in *Tinker*, *Fraser*, and *Kuhlmeier* may seem confusing and contradictory. Do schools really have the authority to monitor and regulate student speech? How certain do school administrators need to be to determine that student expression will cause a "material disturbance" before they take action? How much objectionable student speech must schools tolerate?

When analyzing Internet issues, or any other educational issues for that matter, administrators and teachers must first remember public schools are not responsible for every "bad thing" that happens. Public school educators must follow the same legal standard to which the law holds all human actors: they must behave as ordinary, reasonably prudent persons in their circumstances. The "circumstances" for public school administrators and all educators are simply more exacting—the care and education of children. Being "reasonably prudent" in the context of public education includes learning how to recognize and deal with issues relating to Internet use in public school classrooms and libraries.

Standards for Technology Literacy

Courts will look to prevailing professional standards when judging an educator's actions. In technology matters, several professional organizations have developed standards for technological literacy, which courts will likely look to for guidance. The umbrella organization for technology standards is the International Society for Technology in Education (ISTE), a nonprofit professional organization with worldwide membership. ISTE's *National Educational Technology Standards for Students—Connecting Curriculum and Technology* and *National Standards for Technology in Teacher Preparation* are available for sale through their Web site at http://www.iste.org. In addition, ISTE's Technology Standards for School Administrators (TSSA) collaborative, under the direction of Don Knezek at the University of North Texas, released its official consensus document for school administrators in November 2001. ISTE formally adopted the TSSA consensus document as the *National Educational Technology Standards for Administrators* (NETS*A) in February 2002. NETS*A sets out a list of foundational technology competencies and skills for all administrators, as well as three supplemental, role-specific sets of competencies for administrators with systemic, building-level, or subject-specific responsibilities.

The standards and associated performance indicators require that school administrators assume a leadership role in developing a technology plan for their district. School administrators must project a clear vision for integrating technology into all aspects of education, from teaching to assessment, and foster an environment conducive to realizing that vision. To do this, the TSSA document suggests that administrators must personally apply technology to enhance their own professional practice and to increase both personal and general productivity. Clearly, these standards up the ante for what constitutes technological savvy among educators.

Federal vs. State Law

A second important point to remember is that only federal laws and Supreme Court decisions speak to the country as a whole. Many states have enacted laws that pertain to Internet issues and apply to activities and transactions within that state. Other states may consider them in certain cases, but states are sovereign only over those within their specific jurisdictions. Some laws, such as copyright laws, are federal and apply uniformly nationwide, taking precedence over conflicting state laws.

When judges decide legal questions, they generally interpret and apply either constitutional rights or laws. However, their decisions have different levels of authority and applicability because judges sit in many different courts, state or federal. The state court system includes local and appellate courts, with the State Supreme Court as the state-level court of last resort (except in New York State). Any state court decision is binding only for lower court decisions in the same state. A state court judge in another state may or may not find her out-of-state colleague's decision persuasive in the case before her; she is free to adopt or disregard it.

Similarly, the separate federal court system comprises both local and appellate courts. Cases involving citizens of different states, for example, are brought in federal court. A federal court decision is the controlling authority on lower federal courts in its jurisdiction, but federal judges in different regions or "circuits" may agree or disagree with the ruling.

The U.S. Supreme Court, the highest appellate court in the nation, is the court of last resort for both state and federal cases. Only when the Supreme Court speaks with at least a majority voice does a decision become the controlling precedent for all other courts, state or federal. Even then, the Supreme Court is free to change its collective mind. Moreover, even if the Supreme Court has spoken on an issue, subtle factual nuances may distinguish the deliberations and dictate a different outcome in any given case.

Interpreting Case Citations and Legal References

The importance of determining where a court decision originated is clear. Only by determining a ruling's origin can one tell for whom the decision is binding. Similarly, if someone wants to locate scholarly legal information on a given topic, interpreting journal abbreviations and volume and page notations is critical.

Judges, legal scholars, and good lawyers abide by a style manual containing very specific rules of citation and attribution for cases and other written materials referenced in their decisions, journal articles, and briefs— akin to the various manuals dear to the hearts of high school language arts teachers. The definitive legal style manual is *The Bluebook: A Uniform System of Citation*, published and distributed by the Harvard Law Review Association. The seventeenth edition appeared in 2000.

> Only when the Supreme Court speaks with at least a majority voice does a decision become the controlling precedent for all other courts, state or federal.

The citation rules used by the legal profession are different from, and in most cases use more abbreviations than, the rules formulated by nonlegal scholars. For example, the citation for the "United States Constitution" is simply "CONST." In citing the *Journal of Social Policy*, "Journal" becomes "J.," "Social" becomes "SOC.," and "Policy" becomes "POL'Y." The titles of books and journal articles are always cited in caps, and yes, those second and subsequent letters are printed in a smaller font size. Court decisions, however, are reported in upper and lower case letters. The names of plaintiffs and defendants (or in appeals cases, appellants and appellees) appear first, and are either underlined or italicized. "Versus" is abbreviated simply as "*v.*," not "*vs.*"

The rest of the citation provides the information needed to find the text of the decision. Court cases are usually collected in what are called *reporters*, which can be local, state, federal, or topical. Geographic reporters collect cases originating in different jurisdictions, whereas specialty reporters collect cases dealing with particular topics. For example, the *Atlantic Reporter*, abbreviated

"A.," contains cases from Pennsylvania, New Jersey, and several neighboring states. The *Pacific Reporter*, abbreviated "P.," contains cases from California, Oregon, and other Pacific states. West's *Education Law Reporter*, abbreviated "Ed. Law Rep.," reprints court decisions having special significance for educators and school attorneys. Several reporters are exclusively dedicated to decisions from the federal courts, such as the *Federal Reporter*, abbreviated "F.," or the *Federal Supplement*, abbreviated "F. Supp."

The reporters publish court decisions as they are decided, so the most recent cases appear in the most recent reporters. The first number of a case citation gives the reporter volume; the number after the reporter's abbreviation is the page on which the case begins. As decision after decision was published, the volume numbers of the reporters got higher and higher. Someone eventually said, "Enough!" and started the numbering all over again. To keep things straight, new reporters were designated as "the Second" and eventually even "the Third" series of the given reporter. In keeping with the law's citation brevity, the Second series is designated "2d," and the Third "3d." There are even corresponding rules about how many spaces are allowed between number and reporter abbreviations.

The final part of the case citation identifies the court that decided the case and the year of the decision. For example, the court might be a state court in the Eastern District of Pennsylvania from 1997. The citation would include the following information in parentheses:

(E.D. Pa. 1997)

Or the decision may be from a state appeals court in California, dated 1999. The citation then would be:

(Cal. App. 1999)

If just "Cal." appears, the case is from the California Supreme Court. Similarly, any other state abbreviation indicates that the decision originated in that state's Supreme Court (except for New York State, where, just to confuse everyone, the New York

Supreme Court is *not* the highest court in the state. The state court of last resort in New York is the Court of Appeals).

If the decision originated in a federal Circuit Court of Appeals instead of the state system, the part of the citation in parentheses indicates the specific circuit where the case was decided. For example, a decision from the federal Circuit Court of Appeals in which California is located—the Ninth Circuit—would be designated as such:

(9th Cir. 1999)

The decisions with the most universal applicability—those from the U.S. Supreme Court—are the easiest to cite and to recognize. U.S. Supreme Court decisions appear in several reporters, among them the *United States Reporter*, abbreviated "U.S.," or the *Supreme Court Reporter*, abbreviated "S. Ct." An example of a Supreme Court case citation is *Brown v. Bd. of Educ.*, 347 U.S. 483 (1954).

The Bottom Line

Simply put, quoting a law or a court decision without accompanying citation is not necessarily useful. Context is paramount. Anyone who proffers a law or a court decision out of context to pressure administrators or educators into a given course of action is suspect. Administrators and educators must analyze all information and advice, even that presented here, as reasonably prudent persons and act accordingly, in the Internet-related context as in all other school matters.

Afterword: School Violence and September 11

Unsettled at the present time but increasingly hinted at is the role that the continuing tide of school violence will have on school Internet law. Schools and school students, teachers, and administrators have increasingly become targets of violence, just as the American way of life became a target for terrorism on September 11, 2001. The courts have taken judicial notice of school violence, noting in several cases that the climate of school violence must color judicial analyses of student expression and expressive conduct. The Internet and its attraction to students who are disturbed have figured prominently in several notorious acts of school violence. Such connections are bound to influence contemporary judicial reasoning.

In a larger sense, the perimeters of all American freedoms, especially our rights to free expression and to freedom from governmental searches and seizures, may change as a result of the events of September 11. America's ongoing response to terrorism may influence both legislatures and judges. School administrators and educators must wait and watch to see how terrorism and violence in general will affect school Internet law.

2

Freedom of Expression and the School Internet

ONE OF AMERICANS' MOST CHERISHED AND OFTEN INVOKED FREEDOMS is freedom of expression, a First Amendment right that prevents the government and government agencies from suppressing or stifling speech and other kinds of expression simply because they disagree with or disapprove of its content. When the U.S. Supreme Court struck down parts of the Communications Decency Act in 1997, it explicitly extended First Amendment protection to Internet communications. This ruling has become a mixed blessing for public schools, whose Internet users often have an imperfect understanding of what the First Amendment protects and how it applies in the public school setting.

What the First Amendment Protects— In General

The First Amendment most strongly protects speech or expression that conveys a political message directed to the public in what is called a public forum, that is, a place open to all comers. At the other end of the speech continuum, commercial speech and speech delivered in a nonpublic forum receive less protection. Some forms of speech are completely unprotected, such as "fighting words" and obscenity. Pornography, however, is a protected category of expression, unless it involves child pornography.

What the First Amendment Protects— In Public Schools

The Supreme Court has established that the First Amendment rights of students and teachers in the public school setting are not the same as the rights of adults in nonschool settings. In a series of cases dating back to the Vietnam War era (discussed in Chapter 1), the Court set out fundamental guidelines for ascertaining whether First Amendment protection applies to students' and teachers' school-related expression. Public schools, the Court stated, are *limited* public forums. Students and teachers have the right to free expression in schools unless their expression materially and substantially interferes with the educational process of the school district, or unless such expression would confuse listeners into thinking the message bore the *imprimatur* of the school district.

"Fighting words" and obscenity, of course, receive no First Amendment protection, either inside or outside school. In the special environment of the school, however, lewd, indecent, or offensive speech is also unprotected. Moreover, what is not obscene for adults may constitute obscenity for minors. Public school teachers, as employees of the school district, may have additional restrictions on their freedom of expression, depending on its content. When teachers speak out on matters related to their employment—whether at public meetings or on the Internet—the district has the legal right of an employer to control what they say or write. When teachers speak on matters of public concern, First Amendment protections may apply. However, what constitutes a matter of public concern is sometimes hard to define. Clearly, if a teacher's expression disrupts school operations or interferes with working relationships in the district, the district may suppress that expression. In the school setting, therefore, teachers' First Amendment rights, like those of students, are subordinate to the interests of the school community.

Regulating Expression on the Internet in Schools

The increasing use of the Internet in public schools blurs the distinction between student and teacher speech and expression protected by the First Amendment and expression schools can and should regulate. What do First Amendment protections mean in the school Internet context? Does the First Amendment protect student- or teacher-created Internet communications that criticize school personnel or policies? Does it matter if the communication originated within a school or outside, during school hours or not, on school computers or home computers?

The First Amendment also implicates the corollary to free expression—students' and teachers' right to receive information. The Children's Internet Protection Act of 2000 (CIPA), a subject of ongoing litigation, mandates adoption of *technology protection measures* on all computers purchased with or supported by federal funds to prevent both children under 17 and adults from accessing certain objectionable visual materials on the Internet. Schools and school libraries receiving *e-rate funds* must comply with CIPA. The statute does not specify the nature of the mandatory technology protection measures, but many schools and libraries interpret CIPA to require installation of blocks or filters for certain kinds of Internet material. Censorship in schools and libraries is a sensitive and potentially inflammatory issue. Given that current blocking and filtering software is both text-based and simultaneously over- and under-inclusive, and given that both the American Civil Liberties Union (ACLU) and the American Library Association are vigorously urging the courts to declare that CIPA violates the First Amendment, school districts are in the uncomfortable position of having to comply with CIPA while simultaneously monitoring its progress through the courts.

Limiting Students' In-School Internet Access

Because freedom of expression is a fundamental right guaranteed by the Constitution, any governmental attempt to limit it must be justified by a compelling reason and narrowly tailored to achieve the government's goal. The Internet has the potential to bring educationally inappropriate and disturbing content into the hands of children at the simple click of a computer mouse, and the school district has the right and responsibility to protect children in its care. No commercial software product, however, can deliver the level of narrowly tailored protection constitutionally required. Filtering and blocking technology currently available relies on recognizing predetermined words and phrases, and screening for text offensive in some contexts may also block access to appropriate educational material. Screening the word "homosexual," for example, may limit access to socially acceptable and educationally appropriate information on avoiding HIV/AIDS.

Filtering or Blocking Pictures

Until the Supreme Court declares CIPA unconstitutional, school districts that receive federal funding for telecommunications (e-rate funding and other similar federal money) must implement technology protection measures to protect minors from visual depictions that are (1) obscene, (2) child pornography, or (3) "harmful to minors." Under the statute, minors are children under 17 years old. "Harmful" is broadly defined as depictions of nudity, sex, and excretory bodily functions. CIPA does not mandate filtering of sexually explicit text, only pictures.

The statute also mandates that schools block or filter adults' access to two categories of visual depictions—those that are obscene and child pornography. Administrators, supervisors, and persons authorized by the school may disable the blocking/filtering software to permit unrestricted Internet access for "*bona fide* research or other lawful purposes."

School districts are, therefore, between the rock of CIPA and the hard place of the Constitution, with the threat of discontinuation of federal e-rate funding and computer subsidies if they do not filter Internet access. Moreover, the required filtering of visual images is difficult to accomplish. Resolution of the dilemma is in the hands of the Supreme Court; until it speaks to the issue, districts must comply with CIPA.

Removing Books from the Internet Library

If and when effective and narrowly tailored filtering and blocking technology becomes available, public schools still face the challenge of justifying restrictions of students' freedom to receive information. If the Internet's characterization as a "vast library" is accurate, blocking or filtering Internet access in schools is analogous to removing books from the school library. The Supreme Court noted that public school libraries have "special characteristics" that make them a sensitive environment for issues involving students' freedom of speech. First Amendment concerns arise when public school authorities remove books, even if they only want to protect students from moral dangers and unorthodoxy. School districts may not suppress ideas or impose orthodoxy. To be constitutionally valid, suppression of information available to students in a school library must follow "established, regular, and facially unbiased" procedures for reviewing the educational suitability of the controversial materials. If school authorities do not establish and follow such procedures in filtering students' Internet access, free speech advocates may challenge any actions they take.

> To be constitutionally valid, suppression of information available to students in a school library must follow "established, regular, and facially unbiased" procedures for reviewing the educational suitability of the controversial materials.

Limiting Teachers' In-School Internet Access

If public schools have the right to limit the Internet access of their students to educationally appropriate materials, can they similarly restrict teachers' in-school Internet access? Two recent court decisions pertaining to faculty Internet access at higher education institutions suggest that they may.

In the first case, professors at several of Virginia's state colleges sued the state because their institutions required them to obtain

permission, even for academic research purposes, before accessing sexually explicit Internet materials on state-owned computers.
The professors argued that the rule interfered with their freedom
of expression, but the court viewed the restriction as a simple condition of the professors' employment. Recognizing that the state
has the right as the employer to restrict teachers' expression on
matters relating to their employment, the court upheld the rule.

Approaching the issue from a different perspective, an
Oklahoma court arrived at a similar conclusion. A professor at the
University of Oklahoma brought suit because the university
maintained a dual system of Internet servers. One blocked access
to obscene materials, whereas the other had open access for academic and research purposes. The professor alleged that the dual
system violated his First Amendment rights, by potentially stig-
matizing use of the open access server. The court ruled in favor of
the university. The two-server system remains.

Because teachers are school district employees, the Virginia
and Oklahoma decisions suggest that public school districts may
have greater legal right to limit *teachers'* in-school Internet access
than to limit *students'* access to materials that are not obscene and
not child pornography.

Out-of-School Internet Expression

Concern for the integrity of school operations limits the rights of
students and teachers to express themselves freely in the school
setting. However, what about speech and expression that originate outside school? Do school districts have the right to regulate
student- or teacher-created Internet communications that originate outside the school?

Students' Internet Communications
Students who express negative feelings about their schools or
teachers outside of school may be merely expressing opinions,
and the First Amendment protects such expression. However,
suppose the student publishes his "opinion" on the Web. Is that

protected expression? The courts have not yet resolved this issue definitively, but case law is accumulating in all states.

One widely publicized suit arose after a Missouri high school suspended a student who created an Internet home page that was highly critical of his school administration, inviting readers to call the high school to express their opinions. The student, Brandon Beussink, created the home page on his home computer, after school hours, and the Web site caused no documented disturbance at his school. The principal, however, suspended Beussink for 10 days and ordered him to "clean up" his home page or to "clean it out." The student removed the home page from the Internet and served the suspension, but his suspension caused his grades to drop significantly. The ACLU brought suit on behalf of the student and his parents. The court ruled that the school district had no right to discipline the student simply because it disliked or was upset by the Web site comments.

Pennsylvania courts similarly distinguished between students' out-of-school Web sites that are merely unpleasant or upsetting and Web sites that warrant disciplinary action for their creators. Justin Swidler, a middle school student in the Bethlehem Area School District, made derogatory comments about his algebra teacher and about his principal on his Web pages. The youngster pictured the algebra teacher with her head severed and dripping blood, and solicited contributions to help him hire a "hit man" to kill her. The Web site also morphed his teacher's image into that of Adolf Hitler and called her a "fat bitch." Swidler even accused his principal of having an extramarital affair. The judge noted that the Web site counter indicated that users, most likely other students, accessed the site approximately 234 times before Swidler took it down. He also accepted testimony from both the teacher and principal that they suffered physically and emotionally after viewing the Web site, and that the site interfered with their school-related activities. He concluded that the student's Web site materially disrupted the learning environment in the middle school and that the district was justified in expelling Swidler. A jury awarded the algebra teacher a half of a million dollars in damages, and the principal an undisclosed sum. The case, however, is on appeal to the Pennsylvania Supreme Court.

In some cases, the mere threat of ACLU intervention prompted school boards to reexamine their disciplinary actions. An Ohio school board suspended 11 students from Field High School in Brimfield after they contributed to a gothic Web site they devised. The school board decided not to expel the students after the ACLU became involved. Similarly, a school board in Washington suspended a group of Eastlake High School students who created a Web site called the "Eaztlake Phantom," a popular out-of-school forum for discussion of student issues, after a student from Arizona published a death threat on the site. Again, the school board reversed its decision after the ACLU intervened.

Other cases have resulted in lucrative outcomes, but not for school personnel. An Ohio school board suspended a high school band member, Sean O'Brien, who ran a photo of his band teacher on his home-based Web page, along with insulting personal comments about the teacher. After Sean and his parents sued the district for $550,000 in damages, alleging First Amendment violations, the parents and the district reached an out-of-court settlement in which the district acknowledged that it had "overlooked" the First Amendment and paid Sean and his parents $30,000. A suburban Seattle school board also had to pay after it disciplined a student, Nick Emmett, who posted humorous fake obituaries on the Unofficial Kentlake High Home Page, a Web site he created at home with his father's assistance. Emmett and a fellow student closed the site voluntarily after a reporter interviewed Emmett and suggested that his site was a "hit list," but the high school principal still suspended him for five days. The ACLU of Washington State ultimately negotiated a settlement in which the district agreed to forgo disciplinary action and to pay Emmett's legal fees.

Despite the fact that students' out-of-school Web sites cause heartache and real emotional distress for teachers and administrators named on the sites, and despite the fact that courts have begun to award significant damages to maligned teachers and administrators, students persist in creating and uploading their inflammatory material to the Web. The *Lexington Herald Leader* reported that Metcalfe County High School in Kentucky suspended three high school students in February 2001 for operating a Web site warning about a school disturbance planned by the "Deadly Six" for Valentine's Day. The ACLU reported in July 2001 that it was undertaking the representation of an 8th grade student whom North Canton Middle School in Ohio suspended and placed in an "in-school expulsion" after he created a Web site at home that the school said "bullied" fellow students. Groups of students have even created school gossip Web sites, like the Diamond Ranch High School News, a gossip site run by students in Pomona, California. Teachers and administrators will likely be the continuing butt of such Web sites in the foreseeable future.

Student Hacking

Whereas inflammatory material can sometimes be defended as free expression, criminal acts cannot. In 1998, a court upheld the school district's expulsion of a student, Justin J. Boucher, who authored an underground student newspaper article that described procedures to hack into his high school's central computer system. Computer hacking itself is a criminal act under state and federal laws; however, prosecution of the offense usually requires evidence of actual monetary damages, not simply invasion of the computer system. For example, until recently, the federal antihacking statute required that the prosecution show at least $5,000 in damages caused by the hacking. In Boucher's case, no actual hacking and no monetary damages occurred, but the district suspended the student for a year. Boucher brought suit to bar the expulsion, arguing that his expression was not designed to incite others to criminal acts but was "mere advocacy," protected by the First Amendment. The court ruled that school authorities reasonably foresaw that Boucher's expression would undermine school discipline, and upheld the suspension.

Computer hacking received special attention in Congress after the events of September 11, 2001. The Patriot Act of 2001, signed by President George W. Bush in October 2001, expanded the definition of damages resulting from computer hacking to include threats to public health and safety. F. James Sensenbrenner Jr., chairman of the House Judiciary Committee, expressed his confidence that the expanded definition would increase federal protection against hacking of school Web sites.

Teachers' Personal Internet Expression

Teachers too may receive constitutional protection for Web sites on which they discuss matters of public concern outside of school hours and on their own computers, as long as those sites were not created using school resources. Teachers' expression relating to conditions of their employment, on the other hand, is governed by roughly the same standards that govern students' speech. Districts may take action against teachers whose public or private expression about personal concerns disrupts or materially interferes with the educational operations of the school.

Courts, however, are reluctant to condone prior restraints on expression unless the restraints are content neutral and applied uniformly to all categories of expression and speakers. Applying general First Amendment principles, courts will likely look with disfavor on districts that construct unnecessary roadblocks in advance that chill expression by teachers, even Internet expression. No teachers have yet been challenged to defend their sites in courts.

The Legal Significance of Student Codes of Conduct

Districts with well-articulated discipline policies or codes of student conduct can more forcefully defend their disciplinary actions against students. For example, the Bethlehem Area School District was able to reference its district's Code of Conduct definitions of "disrespect" and "threats/harassment" to defend itself in disciplining Justin Swidler. The court noted that not only had the district defined the prohibited conduct, but it had also communicated its definitions to the student body. The continuing concern about the relationship between students' Internet speech and school violence may also affect both judicial and school district responses. Courts have taken judicial notice of the rising tide of student violence, especially in the context of deciding whether student utterances constitute true threats. The belated discoveries that Columbine High School students Eric Harris and Dylan Klebold had discussed their plans in Internet communications before the actual shootings put school districts on heightened alert for warning signs of student violence. Both courts and school districts may react more harshly to students' critical Internet postings in the wake of such events.

Recommendations for School Districts

Acting with Care

Although the case law involving the First Amendment and school Internet issues is still evolving, school districts can avoid legal liability by following simple, commonsense guidelines. Administrators need to revisit the rationales of the *Tinker, Fraser,* and *Kuhlmeier* decisions (see Chapter 1). Because freedom of expression is such a bedrock principle in American society, school admin-

> Courts have taken judicial notice of the rising tide of student violence, especially in the context of deciding whether student utterances constitute true threats.

istrators must refrain from knee-jerk reactions to situations involving student expression, especially student speech that originates outside of school.

Reprising the Legal Standard

The legal standard is that a student's expression must cause *material and substantial disruption* of school operations or school discipline before the district may take disciplinary action against the student. Furthermore, the district must provide the student with due process, that is, appropriate notice of the consequences of inappropriate or offensive speech *before* the speech occurs, and the opportunity of a hearing after an alleged infraction to determine culpability.

Consequences may be school-imposed or, in the case of statutory violations, involve civil or criminal charges. School-imposed consequences should be explicitly stated and provide an escalating scale of discipline. Penalties should begin by depriving students of their right to participate in extracurricular activities, because no entitlement issues are involved in this kind of discipline.

The more potentially serious the student's offense, the more notice and opportunities for hearings the district must provide. Parents or guardians should be involved at all steps in the process.

District Guidelines and Acceptable Use Policies

School districts need policies that specify what is appropriate student expression and how they will react to inappropriate student expression. The policies and accompanying guidelines must be proactive, not reactive.

School boards and administrators should work together with teachers and parent representatives to formulate age-appropriate guidelines that specifically describe student expression in the school setting or in other areas that will reach or affect the school, such as the Internet. Such guidelines may be part of the school discipline code or a district Internet Acceptable Use Policy (AUP).

Reporting School-Related Web Sites

Districts should also consider adopting policies and procedures that require students and teachers to report Web sites that reference the district or district personnel or activities either favorably or unfavorably, so that the district may monitor them. A simple reporting form should be made available for teachers and students.

Responding with Reason and Caution

Students' misuse of district technology and inappropriate Internet expression may cost school districts dearly, in terms of the financial costs to undo students' technology mischief and the emotional toll on teachers and administrators who are the subject of students' unflattering Web site comments. Districts that have promulgated rules about acceptable use of technology can be comfortable in applying those rules to student hackers. However, districts must adopt a reasoned and cautious approach to disciplining students for out-of-school Internet expression. When students create or post to Web sites critical of the district or staff, administrators should recognize that student Web sites usually disseminate information to a limited audience, predominantly friends of the Web site creator. Publicity concerning objectionable sites only widens that circle.

The First Amendment protects student opinions. Students throughout the history of compulsory education have expressed criticisms of their schools and teachers. Because courts can consider those criticisms to be merely opinions, administrators must carefully consider their responses. One rule of thumb for administrators is to consider how they would react if the criticism were spoken instead of published on the Internet. This "consideration check" might guide administrators to a more reasonable reaction to student Web sites originating and published outside of school.

Keeping Parents in the Loop

If the student's objectionable or offensive message does not threaten the operation or discipline of the school, a telephone call to the appropriate parents or guardians probably should be the first step. Notifying parents may be the most effective discipline. Any administrator or staff member personally defamed or libeled by a student can file criminal or civil charges, but students who merely express their opinions are not automatically liable for defamation under the law. Defamation is a precise legal term that signifies an intentional false communication that exposes the subject of the defamation to "contempt, hatred, ridicule, or obloquy" in a "respectable and considerable part of the community." This is a harsh standard for the court to apply, and one that most students do not achieve in their puerile criticisms and remarks.

Responding to Hacking

Student hackers are a more serious matter. The Supreme Court has vigorously upheld the right of school districts to maintain order in the schools. Hacking is *not* protected expression. School districts should have strong discipline policies in place to deal with computer hacking and provide prominent notice of such policies in student handbooks. Districts should also report all suspected or actual hacking into district servers or computers to the appropriate governmental authorities.

Annotated Legal References

Statutes
- The Children's Internet Protection Act (CIPA) is Public Law 106-554, passed December 21, 2000.
- The Patriot Act, signed into law in October 2001, is Public Law 107-56.

Court Decisions
First Amendment jurisprudence has developed with a long line of U.S. Supreme Court cases. The most important include

- *Abrams v. United States*, 250 U.S. 616 (1919) (Holmes, J., dissenting) (where Justice Holmes enunciated the "marketplace of ideas" rhetoric).
- *Hague v. CIO*, 37 U.S. 496 (1939), and *Lamb's Chapel v. Center Moriches Union Free School District*, 508 U.S. 384 (1993) (where the Court developed the public forum analysis).
- *Chaplinsky v. New Hampshire*, 315 U.S. 568 (1942) (where the Court said "fighting words" are not protected under the First Amendment).
- *Brandenburg v. Ohio*, 395 U.S. 444 (1969) (where the Court refused to allow First Amendment protection for expression that encourages imminent lawlessness).
- *Texas v. Johnson*, 491 U.S. 397 (1989) (holding that desecration of the American flag is protected speech), and *Carey v. Population Services International*, 431 U.S. 678, 701 (1977) (noting that speech cannot be repressed just because it is unpopular).
- *R.A.V. v. City of St. Paul*, 505 U.S. 377 (1992) (where the Court ruled unconstitutional an ordinance that made burning a cross on the lawn of a black family a criminal act, because the ordinance banned only racist "fighting words," not all "fighting words").

Freedom of speech or expression is a fundamental right and, as such, strict scrutiny is the judicial standard of review for alleged unconstitutional restrictions. Under strict scrutiny review, the government must show a compelling interest in the regulation, but the regulation must be narrowly tailored to achieve its goal. "Narrowly tailored" means that the regulation cannot encompass more than is strictly necessary to affect its purpose. The courts will invalidate regulations that are overbroad (*San Antonio Independent School District v. Rodriguez*, 411 U.S. 1 (1973)).

The standards for regulating conduct associated with speech or expression must be well defined. Standards cannot give officials broad discretion in crafting regulations (*Forsythe County v. Nationalist Movement*, 505 U.S. 123 (1992)).

Students' Freedom of Expression and Right to Receive Information. The three seminal U.S. Supreme Court cases establishing the boundaries of students' freedom of expression in K–12 public schools are

- *Tinker v. Des Moines Independent Community School District*, 393 U.S. 503 (1969) (where the Court upheld the rights of students to wear black armbands protesting the Vietnam War, and handed down the often-quoted phrase that "[n]either students [n]or teachers shed their constitutional rights to freedom of speech or expression at the schoolhouse gate").
- *Bethel School District No. 403 v. Fraser*, 478 U.S. 675 (1986) (where the Court upheld the school's suspension of a high school student who repeatedly used graphic and explicit sexual metaphors in a speech at a school assembly for election of class officers).
- *Hazelwood School District v. Kuhlmeier*, 484 U.S. 260 (1988) (where the Court affirmed the school's authority to exercise editorial control over school-sponsored publications, theatrical productions, and other expressive conduct that reasonable observers might attribute to the school or otherwise perceive as bearing the *imprimatur* of the school district).

Also, the U.S. Supreme Court discussed the right of students to receive information in the school setting in *Board of Education v. Pico*, 457 U.S. 853 (1982).

Obscenity and Indecency. The U.S. Supreme Court crafted a definition of what constitutes obscenity in *Miller v. California*, 413 U.S. 15 (1973), and specifically applied the Miller test to Internet materials in *Reno v. ACLU*, 521 U.S. 844 (1997). It was in *Reno v. ACLU* that the Court invalidated sections of the Communications Decency Act of 1996. The U.S. Supreme Court specifically ruled, however, that what is merely indecent for adults may be obscene for children (*Ginsberg v. New York*, 390 U.S. 629 (1968)).

Teachers' Rights to Speak Out. Teachers' rights to speak out are defined in several U.S. Supreme Court decisions, including *Pickering v. Board of Education*, 391 U.S. 563 (1968), *Mount Healthy City School District v. Doyle*, 429 U.S. 274 (1977), and *Connick v. Myers*, 461 U.S. 138 (1983). However, issues of what constitutes matters of public concern necessarily depend on the specific facts in each situation litigated.

Filtering Internet Content. A Virginia court decision that will undoubtedly figure prominently in any litigation over blocking or filtering Internet content is *Mainstream Loudoun v. Board of Trustees of Loudoun County Library*, 2 F. Supp.2d 783, *on remand*, 24 F. Supp.2d 552 (E.D. Va. 1998). The *Loudoun* court analogized filtering Internet content to removing books from a library. Ruling that a public library cannot restrict adult access to material merely because it is unsuitable for children, the court decided that the library's blocking of Internet sites failed the test of being narrowly tailored to achieve a compelling governmental interest.

Two higher education cases dealing with institutions' filtering of faculty access to the Internet, one in Virginia and one in Oklahoma, may figure in future court decisions about filtering issues at the K–12 level. The Supreme Court has recently refused to overturn the decision of the Fourth Circuit in the Virginia case (*Urofsky v. Gilmore*, 216 F.3d 401 (4th Cir. 2000)), and the Tenth Circuit has affirmed the earlier Oklahoma district court decision (*Loving v. Boren*, 956 F. Supp. 953 (W.D. Okla. 1997), *aff'd* 133 F.3d 771 (10th Cir. 1998)).

Students' Out-of-School Internet Expression. Following are the case citations for the Web sites and student Internet communications discussed in the text:

- *Beussink v. Woodland R-IV School District*, 30 F. Supp.2d 1175 (E.D. Mo. 1998) (where the student outside of school created a Web site critical of his school and its administration).
- *Boucher v. School Board of School District of Greenfield*, 134 F.3d 821 (7th Cir. 1998) (where the student wrote an article instructing readers how to "hack into" his school's computer system).
- *Emmett v. Kent School District No. 415*, 92 F. Supp.2d 1088 (W.D. Wash. 2000) (where the student's out-of-school Web site contained humorous fake obituaries of school officials).
- *J.S. v. Bethlehem Area School District*, 757 A.2d 412 (Pa. Cmwlth. 2000) (where the court upheld the school district's discipline of a middle school student whose Web site solicited money to hire a hit man to kill his algebra teacher). The *J.S.* decision is currently on appeal to the Pennsylvania Supreme Court.

3

Privacy and the School-Sponsored Internet

WHEN STUDENTS ACCESS THE INTERNET EITHER IN SCHOOL OR OUTSIDE school, educators want to be sure that students communicate appropriately and share information safely. Internet users cannot control where posted messages ultimately go or who might read them. Anyone can create hyperlinks to posted messages, carrying them far beyond their intended recipients. Internet sites that collect information about visitors can also sell that information, or pass it along freely, without notification or permission.

Protecting Children Under 13

Concerned about the ease with which Web site operators might obtain personal information from unsuspecting children, Congress passed the Child Online Privacy Protection Act (COPPA) in 1998. COPPA is the only federal legislation that regulates collection of personal information online. The law protects children under the age of 13 from the unauthorized and deceptive collection of personal information from them by Web site operators and Internet service providers (ISPs). All Web site operators and ISPs who have *actual knowledge* that the person from whom they seek information is a child must notify the child's parents and obtain parental consent before collecting, using, or disclosing personal information about the child. COPPA became effective April 21, 2000. So far, contrary to the fate of other Internet legislation, no one has challenged COPPA in the courts. The Federal Trade Commission has used COPPA to prevent at least one failed e-business from selling customer lists containing personal information about minors. Unfortunately, the wording of the statute requiring Web site operators to have actual knowledge that the individual providing information is a child under 13 may shield Web site operators who argue that they "didn't know" the information provider was a child. COPPA is not complete protection.

Cookies—More Than Just Calories

Aside from the information that users willingly or unwillingly provide to Web site operators, Internet protocols enable Web site servers to "tag" the computers of Internet users who visit particular sites. Called *cookies*, these tags attach to the hard drives of users' computers and make it quicker and easier for a computer's operating system to access a given site in the future, but they also silently track Web site visits. Cookies may enable site operators to combine information from separate databases to construct personal profiles of Internet users, and to exchange user information for marketing purposes. Cookies on the hard drives of school computers can also communicate aggregate information about the Internet preferences of students and staff who log on to school computers. Examination of the cookies on particular hard drives can also give school districts information about how particular computers are being used.

Privacy on District and School Web Sites

Many school districts, individual schools, teachers, parents' groups, and even school athletic teams have Web sites. A school presence on the Web can be a vehicle for communication with parents as well as a source of positive public relations and pride for the entire community. The school or district Web site can also function to support internal communications among students and staff. If the school district or any of its employees post personally identifiable student information on a Web site directly or indirectly maintained by the district, however, the posted information can trigger legally enforceable privacy causes of action.

The Family Educational Rights and Privacy Act

Americans value their privacy, and invasions of privacy can create both criminal and civil liability. Federal and state laws protect student and family privacy. School districts that receive federal funding must comply with the federal Family Educational Rights and Privacy Act (FERPA). FERPA requires that school districts provide parents and students over 18 with annual notice of their rights to inspect their children's or their own education records and to have that information kept confidential.

FERPA also prevents schools from releasing students' education records without written parental consent, except in certain limited circumstances. The courts have not yet articulated exactly what constitutes an *education record*. The Tenth Circuit Court of Appeals, in ruling on an Oklahoma mother's complaint about grading practices in her daughter's 6th grade class, decided that peer grading of students' papers violated FERPA because the students' grades are education records that the teacher should not allow students to share. On February 19, 2002, the Supreme Court reversed the Tenth Circuit in *Owasso Independent School District No. I-011 v. Falvo*, declining to upset the balance between the responsibilities of states and the federal government in operating America's schools. The court ruled that peer grading and calling out students' grades in the classroom for the teacher to record does not violate FERPA.

Although the *Owasso* decision means that teachers in Colorado, Kansas, New Mexico, Oklahoma, Utah, and Wyoming—the states in the Tenth Circuit—can resume the practice of allowing students to grade each other's assignments, the decision is perhaps more important because of the issues it did not resolve. For example, FERPA does not explicitly state that private individuals can sue to enforce the statute's provisions. The Oklahoma mother, Kristja Falvo, had alleged that in violating

FERPA, the district had violated her children's civil rights. The Supreme Court did not decide whether FERPA provides a party with a cause of action enforceable under the 1964 federal civil rights statute, 42 U.S.C. § 1983.

Secondly, the Supreme Court did not decide when a test grade or student assignment grade actually becomes an education record protected under FERPA. The justices limited their ruling to determining that neither peer-graded schoolwork nor the calling out of peer-determined grades constitutes education records under FERPA. And finally, the justices also specifically declined to decide the broader question of whether the peer grades, once recorded by the teacher, are education records or whether a classroom teacher's gradebook itself is an education record. These issues will surely arise again in future FERPA challenges and enforcements.

Just as the Supreme Court pointedly limited its *Owasso* decision, other courts have also spoken very narrowly to specific factual issues in FERPA cases. Especially in the Internet context, many uncertainties about the scope and applicability of FERPA remain. For example, the following may all qualify as privacy violations under FERPA if posted on district-supported and district-maintained Internet Web sites:

- Personally identifiable school information about particular students,
- Identifiable student work, and
- Identifiable student communications posted in district-maintained chat rooms.

Directory Information

What kind of student information *can* districts or schools safely post on their Web sites? FERPA permits school districts to release *directory information* about students—provided that they publicly notify parents about what the district considers to be directory information and that they give parents an opportunity to opt out of having their children's directory information released without written permission. Standard examples of directory information include student names and addresses, telephone numbers, schools attended, grade levels, and honors and awards received. Directory information may also include student photographs, e-mail addresses, or information about students' participation in athletics.

School districts have the power under FERPA to determine what information they consider to be directory information. The public notice of what the district classifies as directory information can be a newspaper notice or a notice in the school or district handbook. The district must also notify parents of their right to prevent the release of their children's directory information and of the time frame in which parents must indicate their written desire to opt out of release of all or part of the information.

> School districts have the power under FERPA to determine what information they consider to be directory information.

Before releasing any nondirectory information that might identify a certain student, districts must obtain specific written consent from parents. The consent must specify the records to be released, the reason they will be released, and to whom they will be released. The district's annual FERPA notice or a blanket release form signed by parents at the beginning of the school year is not legally sufficient to shield the district from liability if it releases nondirectory information during the school year.

With the Internet's availability, the ease and low cost of uploading student information to the Web, the attractiveness of youngsters and adolescents photographed in school settings, and the eagerness of school officials for positive publicity, the temptation to "forget" FERPA is great. Aside from inviting liability under the statute, however, posting information that identifies a specific student and gives information about that student's whereabouts could attract child predators or facilitate child custody violations. Districts should not want to do either.

Parents' Rights to Access School Internet Logs

If a school district monitors the Internet use of its students, may parents or guardians access copies of district Internet records? A convincing argument can be made that they may do so. If school districts provide student Internet access, they assume the responsibility for supervising students' use of that resource on school-supported computers. Parents have the right to see if that supervision is being exercised appropriately; however, they do *not* have the right to private information about particular students other than their own children or about school employees.

State *sunshine laws* may require districts to provide parents with not only information about their children's Internet use, but also statistical information about school-supported Internet use. This information may include statistics about the frequency and duration of student visits to pornographic sites, employees' Internet shopping excursions, and other noneducational uses of the taxpayer-supported Internet in public schools. School districts have encountered parent demands to release district logs of student Internet use and even e-mail communications sent to the district by district residents weighing in on controversial issues before the school board. Because sunshine laws are at issue, districts that delete electronic records in an attempt to circumvent disclosure may be liable.

School districts may also encounter parent demands to release details of the programs they use to filter or block objectionable Internet content. Current federal filtering legislation mandates filtering and blocking certain objectionable visual images (see Chapter 2). Under the Children's Internet Protection Act (CIPA), parents and community taxpayers have the right to watchdog school districts' compliance with laws enacted to protect children in schools from harmful Internet content.

If districts require parents to give permission for their children to access the Internet in school, parents may have an even more persuasive argument that schools must allow them access to school Internet logs. Parents may seek assurances that schools adequately supervise their children's Internet use; they have the power to rescind their permission and prohibit school Internet access for their children. Enhanced record keeping may thereby become the schools' responsibility. Because parental scrutiny of school Internet logs could potentially reveal inadequacies in teacher supervision of student Internet users, school districts have encountered union demands for district-sponsored liability insurance for teachers.

State Privacy Laws

State laws also protect personal privacy. States generally recognize four aspects of what is called the tort of privacy:

- **Misappropriation of likeness.** A school district is liable for committing this aspect of the privacy tort if it posts on a Web site without authorization a likeness of a student or staff member that has commercial value unrelated to school attendance; for example, the likeness of a student athlete who receives compensation for endorsements.
- **Public disclosure of private facts.** The private facts disclosed must be facts that would reasonably cause embarrassment, even if true. Disseminating information about a student's medical or psychological condition in a confidential e-mail that either purposely or inadvertently becomes public may be such a tort.
- **Portraying a person in a false light.** The manner of portrayal would have to be such that a reasonable person would find it objectionable. For example, if the school district falsely portrayed a teacher as a neat, well-dressed role model, a reasonable teacher would have no cause to object. This would not violate the teacher's privacy. However, e-mails that portray a staff member in offensive or unflattering language, even if sent in confidence, may allow for a cause of action.
- **Intrusion on seclusion.** A person can allege intrusion on seclusion even if personal information or photographs were merely collected and never actually published. Parents may feel that posting photographs of students in special education settings or uploading identifiable student work produced during special education classes discloses private facts or intrudes on their seclusion.

State laws give slightly different nuances to the definitions of each separate tort action, and districts must obtain specific legal information about their particular state privacy laws.

Defamation in Internet Communications

The privacy tort of portraying someone in a false light is closely related to defamation and libel. Defamation is an intentional false communication that injures another's reputation or good name. It can be published, in which case it is libel, or spoken, which is slander. The essence of defamation is that it diminishes the respect and esteem others feel for a person, and subjects the person to ridicule, disgrace, or contempt. If the defamation is directed at a public official, it must be made with "malicious intent," i.e., with the intent to inflict injury, without justification or excuse.

Suing for Defamation

Can school district employees bring a defamation or libel suit against a student who makes actionable comments about them on a Web site? Moreover, is the district liable if the defamatory communication is created on the school-supported Internet?

The first question is interesting because defamation is a false communication; truth is an affirmative defense to an allegation of defamation. When students create Web sites that insult school administrators or teachers, some shred of truth may instigate the comments. Administrators or teachers may have a cause of action for defamation or libel, but in many cases, bringing that cause to court may be an acute source of embarrassment. A lawsuit may open the proverbial can of worms. An educator's history of psychological problems, an unflattering classroom evaluation, a messy divorce—all could be fair game in the discovery process allowed by the law. Only in the most egregious cases would a defamation or libel suit seem an appropriate response to an offensive student Web site.

The question of suing students for defamation is also interesting because at least one court distinguished students' potentially defamatory statements from statements of opinion. Suppose the student's Web site comments include statements that a teacher "sucks" or that a principal is a "lousy" administrator. A student has neither the professional experience nor the educational credentials to make substantive judgments as to teacher or administrator

competency; therefore, a court may find that such insulting statements are merely statements of opinion and, as such, protected by
the First Amendment.

Liability for Defamation

Whether the district is liable when students use the school-supported Internet to post truly defamatory communications may
depend on the extent of supervision and control a district can reasonably bring to bear on users of its Internet services. The
Supreme Court has ruled that an Internet service provider
(ISP) is not liable for defamatory communications posted
by users of its services; ISPs are mere conduits of their sub-
scribers' communications. The Court in *Lunney v. Prodigy
Services Company* also declined to hold the ISP negligent for
failing to supervise communications on its site because the
job of supervising its "countless" users was too much to impose.

> The question of suing students for defamation is also interesting because at least one court distinguished students' potentially defamatory statements from statements of opinion.

The courts have not specifically ruled that public schools are
ISPs, and most public schools do not supply Internet services to
"countless" students. In the context of the numerous and diverse
responsibilities of school districts, however, districts may be
excused from the responsibility for defamatory or offensive communications that make their way onto their Web pages, as long as
the district takes reasonable steps to supervise the Web site's overall content.

Privacy Issues in E-mail

The discussion of privacy issues so far has studiously avoided
mention of school-supported e-mail. In order for a student, educator, or parent to claim violation of a legally recognizable privacy

concern, that person must have a reasonable expectation of privacy. The law recognizes no expectation of privacy in school-supported e-mail. Does this mean schools have no legal worries or responsibilities in the context of student or staff e-mail? Schools do not escape so easily. E-mail privacy concerns will be addressed in Chapter 6.

Recommendations for Schools

Policies, Not Paranoia

School district privacy policies are not a sign of paranoia; they are essential in today's Internet environment. District Internet-related privacy policies should be included in each school handbook and disseminated not only to students, but also to parents, staff, and community members. Privacy rights should be addressed in the district's Acceptable Use Policy (AUP) for the Internet. Before formulating privacy policies, districts must decide what student and parent information they will collect, what they will share online, and what they will do with information they neither need nor want.

Cookie Policies

Cookies have not received a great deal of attention in the school technology literature. They are a reality, however, and at the very least districts should have a conversation about their existence on school computers. Cookies can be removed from hard drives. Districts need to decide whether to allow cookies to accumulate on computers or whether to periodically remove them. Districts also need to decide what they will do, if anything, with the information the cookies provide about use of a particular district computer. More information about cookies and cookie removal can be found on the Web site of the Electronic Privacy Information Center at http://www.epic.org.

Centralizing Control to Comply with FERPA

School districts violate FERPA when they have a policy or practice of releasing personally identifiable student information without written parental permission. The Internet makes this so easy to do. A single release of student information without permission is not a violation of FERPA; however, the ire of even one parent who objects to the release of information can exhaust the time and patience of a school administrator. Moreover, in a district with many schools and with Web pages designed by many hands, incidents of inappropriate releases of student information—one here, one there—can easily add up to a practice of unlawful action.

Perhaps the most important step a district can take to ensure its compliance with FERPA, and thereby protect itself and its students, is to centralize the uploading of information to all of the school-run Web sites in the district. A school district that relinquishes control of content on district-supported Web sites is asking for trouble. The person in charge should be a technology specialist, conversant with FERPA and other federal legislation such as the Copyright Act of 1976 and its subsequent amendments, especially the Digital Millennium Copyright Act (see Chapter 5). Ideally, the person in charge is also a competent editor, with expertise in grammatical construction.

Deciding What Is Directory Information

The district needs to determine what it will consider to be directory information and promulgate the list of items with specific instructions to parents about how they can opt out of having their children's information published. Although FERPA allows this notice to be given in a simple newspaper advertisement, and districts may be tempted to promulgate this information on their Web sites, districts need to examine the demographics of their populations. Do all residents have reliable access to Internet communications? Fair opportunity for notice requires that the notice reaches all parents who might want to exercise their rights to opt out.

Getting Permission to Post

Districts must adopt and implement a policy about publishing student work and photographs on the Internet that is consistent with FERPA. Student work that is identifiable as produced by or belonging to an individual student should not be uploaded to the district-supported Web pages unless the parent gives specific written permission. The same applies to student photographs. Blanket parent permissions do not necessarily satisfy FERPA when districts release personally identifiable student information. Student work may be personally identifiable even if the student's name is not attached to the work. If the student work can be considered directory information—for example, if it is an award, *and* the district has included awards in its list of directory information, *and* the parent did not opt out of such publication—then publication of student award information is proper under FERPA.

Public folders in which students post works in progress, district-sponsored chat rooms, and even e-mail that can be identified as belonging to a specific student may all be protected under FERPA if the district maintains the folders and other avenues of communication. Obtaining parental consent for students' participation in these online experiences is the district's safest course of action.

State Privacy Laws

State privacy laws may also apply in given situations. Districts should instruct their solicitors to research state privacy laws and check district privacy policies to ensure compliance.

Forestalling Offensive Communications

Districts can take proactive measures to avoid defamation issues. District AUPs should clearly state that the district will not tolerate offensive student communications produced or promulgated through district-supported computers. The consequences for students who disregard the AUP should be clearly spelled out and explicitly reference the district student code of conduct or the student discipline code, as appropriate. The policy should also prohibit and address the consequences of offensive student Internet communications originating outside of school that disrupt the education of students.

Districts should also put employees on notice that school-supported technology is to be used solely for educational purposes. Consequences of noneducational uses by staff may be negotiated and included in collective bargaining agreements.

Annotated Legal References

Statutes

- The Family Educational Rights and Privacy Act of 1974 (FERPA) appears in the U.S. Code as 20 U.S.C. § 1232g. FERPA is also known as the Buckley Amendment.
- The federal Civil Rights Act is 42 U.S.C.A. § 1983. Plaintiffs often seek a cause of action for deprivation of rights guaranteed under this statute, one of several enacted to guarantee freedom from discrimination after the American Civil War in the mid-1800s.
- The Child Online Privacy Protection Act (COPPA) is Public Law 105-277, passed October 2, 1998.
- The Children's Internet Protection Act (CIPA) is Public Law 106-554, passed December 21, 2000.

Court Decisions

- The Supreme Court declined to impose liability on an ISP for defamatory postings by a subscriber in *Lunney v. Prodigy Services Co.*, 701 N.Y.S.2d 684 (1999).
- The Federal Trade Commission invoked the Child Online Privacy Protection Act (COPPA) to prevent the bankrupt company Toysmart.com from selling its mailing lists and information about children's toy preferences in *Federal Trade Commission v. Toysmart.com, Inc.*, No. 00-1134-RGS (D. Mass., Jul. 21, 2000).
- The judicial decision extending FERPA protection to peer-graded student papers as education records in the states of the Tenth Circuit (Colorado, Kansas, New Mexico, Oklahoma, Utah, and Wyoming), *Falvo v. Owasso Independent School District No. I-011*, 233 F.3d 1203 (10th Cir. 2000), received certification to proceed to the U.S. Supreme Court on June 25, 2001. Eight months later the Supreme Court reversed the Tenth Circuit in *Owasso Independent School District No. I-011 v. Falvo*, 122 S. Ct. 934 (2002). According to the Supreme Court, peer-graded student assignments are not education records protected under FERPA.

4

The Basics of Copyright Law

As the previous chapters discussed, judges do not always agree about how the First Amendment applies to public school-related Internet issues. Copyright law, although seemingly straightforward, has its own set of uncertainties when applied to public school Internet issues.

Conflicting Copyright Goals

The basic notion of copyright embodies a tension between the public's right to access and build on the creative works of authors and the proprietary rights of authors to control the use of their creations. When authors publish their work in printed form or upload and display their work on the Internet, are they not putting it "out there" to be seen and used? The answer is "it depends."

The basic question in copyright law is who has the right to do what with an author's work, whether that work is in traditional, hard copy format or on the Internet. The federal Copyright Act of 1976 applies to both. However, educators need to be aware of recent amendments and judicial decisions that directly affect how they and their students recognize and use copyrighted material, and what school libraries can and must do with material not yet in the public domain.

Copyright vs. Plagiarism

Copyright infringement is separate and distinct from plagiarism. Students and teachers who copy material from any sources without attribution are guilty of plagiarism. In order for a copyright violation to occur, the work being copied must have an active copyright. Plagiarism, on the other hand, can occur with *any* work, including those in the public domain. Most published works, either traditional or online, are protected by copyright, but the copyright holder may be difficult to ascertain because copyright notice is no longer required.

Copyright: How It Works

Before 1976, the process of copyrighting a work was clear-cut. All an author had to do was publish his work with the familiar "©" copyright notice attached, and the work was protected for 28 years. Since Congress passed the Copyright Act of 1976, however, federal copyright protection attaches automatically to all original works at the moment they are fixed in a tangible medium of expression, whether published or unpublished. A student's original poem or research paper—even a teenager's diary tucked in a secret drawer— is copyright protected under federal law from the moment of its creation. No one but the creator of the work has the right to reproduce the work in any form, to distribute it, or to make derivative works based on it, except in certain limited cases described below.

The 1976 Copyright Act also changed the term of copyright protection to a life-based system, granting protection for the life of the author plus 50 years. A 1998 amendment extended the term of protection to life plus 70 years, although the Supreme Court may weigh in soon to negate this extension.

Copyright Notice Not Required

The American copyright landscape changed even more dramatically after the United States signed the Berne Convention, an international agreement to reduce the formalities associated with copyright. Berne makes copyright notice optional for all works created after March 1, 1989. As a result, educators cannot assume that a work is in the public domain just because it lacks a copyright notice.

What Is and Is Not Copyrightable

Besides protecting the original writings of authors, copyright also extends to works written anonymously and with pseudonyms and to important categories of nonwritten works. Copyright protects the following types of expression:

- Literary, musical, and dramatic works;
- Pantomimes and choreographic works;
- Pictorial, graphic, and sculptural works;
- Motion pictures and other audiovisual works;
- Sound recordings; and
- Architectural works.

Some works, however, are *not* copyrightable. Most importantly, ideas and facts are not copyrightable; only the particular, original way an author chooses to express them is protected. Examples of noncopyrightable works include

- Slogans,
- Short phrases,
- Titles of works,
- Names of literary characters,
- Industrial designs,
- Typeface designs, and
- Listings (such as telephone directories) or forms (like ledger sheets).

Other forms of government-enforced protections may be available for these noncopyrightable works. For example, patents are available for certain designs. Similarly, trademarks may protect certain slogans and phrases considered too short to be copyrightable.

Government Documents

The federal government itself cannot hold a copyright. Therefore, federal documents, federal government publications, and federal court decisions are *not* protected by copyright. Anyone may freely copy government documents like statutes, ordinances, regulations, and judicial opinions.

Copyright and Technology

Computer programs are copyrightable. Although a 1980 addition to the Copyright Act authorizes computer program owners, such as school districts, to make archival or backup copies, district employees who copy programs for other purposes or share backup copies violate copyright law. In addition, district employees who upload unauthorized copies of computer programs, even for educational purposes, infringe on copyright. School districts have been fined for this kind of software piracy.

The Digital Millennium Copyright Act of 1998

In 1998, Congress updated the Copyright Act with the Digital Millennium Copyright Act (DMCA) to deal with new technologies like the Internet. Not all of DMCA pertains to schools or school Internet issues, but school districts need to pay attention to the following provisions:

- **Title I.** Title I makes it a crime to circumvent antipiracy measures built into most commercial software. Interestingly, DMCA makes an exception for Internet users who "burn off" or remove cookies from their computers. (Cookies are identification tags that can track Internet site visits. See Chapter 3.) DMCA also allows librarians to circumvent piracy protections in order to preview materials they might want to purchase.
- **Title II.** Title II, also called the Online Copyright Infringement Liability Limitation Act, protects Internet service providers (ISPs) from being sued in certain cases for monetary damages if clients using their services violate copyright. Under the law, an ISP can take advantage of this *safe harbor* provision in four situations:

1. When the ISP acts merely as a passive conduit for information, neither selecting, editing, nor directing the transmitted information;
2. When the ISP stores information on networks or users' hard drives in order to speed up future access to the same information (so-called *system caching*);
3. When ISP users, not the ISP itself, copy and store copyrighted information on hard drives or networks; and
4. When ISP search engines direct users to locations where copyrighted material is used illegally.

School Districts as ISPs

Section 512 of DMCA refers to "nonprofit educational institutions" and defines an ISP very broadly as a provider of online services or network access or the operator of such facilities, but stops short of specifically identifying public school districts as ISPs. No case has yet come before the courts on this issue. Public school districts should note that if the courts decide they are service providers under DMCA, the law protects them from having to pay monetary damages for copyright infringements by its users as long as the district

- Is unaware of infringing activities by its users;
- Does not profit financially from them;
- Adopts and reasonably implements a policy of terminating service for repeat copyright violators; and
- Discourages its users from interfering with technology protection measures, such as copy prevention measures.

In addition, the ISP must designate on its Web site an individual to whom visitors can report copyright violations and agree to remove infringing material when notified properly. The U.S. Copyright Office has an optional form with which to register this person. The form is available at www.loc.gov/copyright/onlinesp/ and requires a $20 fee for listing this information on the Copyright Office Web site. The DMCA safe harbor provision for ISPs has been tested and upheld in the courts by several commercial Internet service providers.

Other DMCA Provisions Important for School Districts

Another part of DMCA applies to computer hardware repair and maintenance operations. Computer technicians, who must copy portions of computer programs into RAM in order to effect computer hardware repairs, are not liable for copyright infringement simply because of the copying.

DMCA also relaxes the proscriptions for copying copyrighted works for librarians in nonprofit libraries, allowing them to make up to three digital copies of a work for preservation or interlibrary loan purposes. These copies cannot be distributed to the public except for use inside the library.

If a work's format has become obsolete, librarians may also archive or copy deteriorating works in new formats not available at the time of the original work's creation. A school-related example could be deteriorating film loops copied onto videotapes or CD-ROMs. Librarians, however, must put the appropriate copyright notice on all copies.

Copyright Infringement

Anyone who makes an unauthorized copy of a copyrighted work, including uploading it to or downloading it from the Internet, is potentially liable for copyright infringement. Copyright infringement does not require intent or any particular state of mind; as such, it is a strict liability offense. Penalties for copyright infringement are severe, including court-ordered destruction of infringing articles, reimbursement of lost profits to the author, or money damages up to $150,000 per infringing event or article, with the possible tripling of this amount in certain cases. Criminal penalties are also possible, including jail time. In some cases even attorneys' fees are part of the penalty.

Assigning Liability

Because copyright notice is optional, ascertaining if a work is protected or in the public domain can sometimes be tricky, especially for works on the Internet. The "innocent infringer" doctrine may protect students and teachers who unintentionally violate copyright. In the case of alleged infringement by a student or teacher, moreover, the copyright owner may have no financial incentive to sue. If the school district, however, enables students or teachers to access and copy protected documents by providing Internet services, the holder of a copyright could pursue redress from the deep pockets of a school district on a theory of vicarious liability. Whether DMCA will provide a safe harbor for the district is uncertain.

Fortunately, before a copyright holder can win a suit for vicarious liability against a school district, he must prove that the school district had the right and ability to control the acts of the person or people who actually infringed the copyright and that the school district realized a direct financial benefit from the infringement.

Although school districts unquestionably have the *right* to control users of its online services, their *ability* to control sophisticated student Internet users is questionable. Unless the school district benefits financially from the infringement, however, a finding of vicarious liability is unlikely. Defending against any lawsuit is expensive. The only prudent alternative for a school district is to direct educators, staff, and students to assume that all works, with the exception of federal government documents, are copyright protected unless the materials clearly state that they may be freely copied.

Browsing and Downloading

Where does this leave school districts? Browsing an Internet document involves copying the document to a computer's RAM. Downloading an Internet document is copying the work from the computer screen to a hard drive. Does this mean that browsing or downloading a copyrighted Internet document is a copyright violation?

Courts generally agree that copying to RAM is analogous to forming a brain image of written material, what the courts call "the functional equivalent of reading" by humans who cannot perceive digital information any other way. Internet browsing, therefore, does not violate copyright. The very nature of the Internet requires copying of data at many nodes of the network. This is not the kind of copying that school districts need to worry about.

Both teachers and students, however, are accustomed to searching for current, educationally relevant information on the Internet. Students use this material in reports and research papers, sometimes excerpting substantial chunks of unchanged text and graphics. Teachers upload student work to the Internet, many times without prior permission from students or parents; they are also accustomed to downloading and reproducing works for classroom use. Chapter 5 more fully discusses possible copyright infringement in schools and fair use of copyrighted materials in schools.

Recommendations for Schools

Materials on the Internet are so accessible and easy to download that many people assume they are free for the taking. That, of course, is not the case. Copyright laws apply to Internet materials with the same force as to "hard copy" materials. Although the likelihood of anyone suing an individual teacher or student over copyright infringement for downloading, forwarding, or otherwise distributing limited copies of copyrighted materials is slim, school districts should not be cavalier about condoning such practices. Districts also need to be careful about their employees or students uploading copyrighted material to district Web sites or establishing unauthorized caches or links that violate copyright. In addition, districts need to take measures to prevent anyone associated with the district from publishing students' and staff members' copyrighted works on the Internet without their permission.

Mounting a Program of Copyright Education

The first and best preventive measure a school district can take is to devise, adopt, and implement an ongoing education program for employees, students, parents, and district volunteers that sets out the facts about copyright law and guidelines for handling copyrighted materials. Programs can include teacher inservice workshops, articles in school newsletters, specially prepared pamphlets or leaflets, signs on duplicating machines, or information posted on the district Web site. Districts also can provide intensive training for selected administrators and master teachers, who then can travel among district schools to give short, informative talks at school faculty meetings and parent-teacher meetings. Informing and raising the consciousness of staff about copyright issues, however, is just the start.

Developing and Adopting a Board Copyright Policy

The school board should give serious consideration to adopting a copyright policy containing the following elements:

- A short and succinct statement of how a work acquires copyright, how to recognize copyrighted materials, and what copyright actually means for a given work. Many teachers, parents, and students simply do not know that copyright notice is not required on copyrighted works.
- An explanation of fair use (see Chapter 5).
- The guidelines for fair use as it relates to duplicating and using copyrighted materials in the classroom.

The policy should also specifically state that copyright applies to text and graphics in digital format, computer programs and materials accessed via the Internet, as well as traditional media such as books, pamphlets, plays, musical scores, and movies.

Promulgating Guidelines Widely

If the district publishes a technology manual for staff, the copyright policy should be included. The policy should also be referenced in teachers' collective bargaining documents, student handbooks, and parent newsletters. Details of the dissemination of the policy should be archived with the policy and updated when appropriate.

The district should also consider devising a sample form with which teachers and other staff can request permission to use copyrighted hard copy or online materials. These forms should be on district letterhead and made available at the district office and at each school building in the district. They should be stored along with a directory of publishers and their addresses and the address of the Copyright Clearance Center, from whom permission to use copyrighted works often can be obtained. Many Web sites post an e-mail address where requests for reprint permission can be sent; district staff should be alerted to look for such information.

Including Copyright Guidelines in the District Code of Conduct

In addition to formulating an official school board policy on copyright and intellectual property, boards, district administrators, and classroom teachers must work together to flesh out and incorporate the policy into the overall district code of conduct. Procedures should be specified that incorporate the following points:

- Clear and actual notice of what is expected of district employees and students using technology in the school setting;
- A comprehensive explanation of the consequences of misusing technology provided in the school context, including Internet connectivity; and
- The degree of due process that will be afforded to students or employees who fail or refuse to comply with the policy's expectations of behavior. At a minimum, due process requires notice and an opportunity for a hearing. The more serious the nature of the violation, the more thorough the due process required.

As part of this fleshing out, school authorities and teachers must work with knowledgeable members of the community to proactively investigate the capabilities of any technology whose use the school board authorizes, funds, or supports in the district. They must anticipate and identify potential abuses, educationally inappropriate applications, or illegal conduct that may result from implementing such technology.

Putting a One Policy/One Person Rule in Place

The district administration or school board should designate one district official to control, monitor, and approve any uploading of material or linking to the district Web site. This official, who should be known by all district personnel, should be under the direct supervision of the superintendent. The district also should specify uniform, confidential procedures for reporting the misuse of district computer resources and violations of copyright to a centralized office or district official. Finally, the district should ensure that all personnel are on notice that the policies and rules apply to *all* district employees, and that the district will vigorously prosecute any violations, no matter who commits them.

Internet Acceptable Use Policies and Copyright

Internet User Agreements or Acceptable Use Policies (AUPs), which will be discussed briefly here and more fully in Appendix A, are extremely important. As strategic documents, they can be used by districts to accomplish the dual goals of providing notice of expected behavior and the consequences of misbehavior. An explicit statement in the AUP should reference the district's code of conduct, making a violation of the AUP a violation of the code. At a minimum, AUPs should state

- The district's expectation that district computing facilities will be used exclusively for educational purposes;
- The district's expectations that students and teachers will use educationally appropriate speech and expression when using the Internet and other technological tools;
- Users' responsibilities to avoid copyright violations;

- Users' reasonable expectations (or lack of such expectations) of privacy in any and all uses of district technology resources; and
- Users' responsibilities to avoid substantial and material disruption of the educational process for the school community.

These general guidelines should be expanded in language readily comprehensible for students and teachers, and include specific examples of the proscribed conduct. A nonexhaustive list of examples of prohibited behavior may include the following:

- Accessing educationally inappropriate Internet materials;
- Using the Internet or school district e-mail for noneducational purposes;
- Tampering with computer operating systems;
- Hacking into district programs;
- Violating the integrity of district servers;
- Violating copyright;
- Plagiarizing;
- Sending or forwarding inappropriate, vulgar, indecent, or harassing e-mail;
- Caching or linking in violation of copyright; and
- Posting personally identifiable information about self or peers to school-related Web sites.

If AUPs include such examples, a disclaimer should be added stating that the list of prohibited behaviors is not exhaustive and is offered for illustration only. All terms mentioned in the AUP, such as "vulgar," "indecent," and "harassing," should be carefully and specifically defined in an appended glossary that is prominently referenced.

Should a district require teachers and students to sign AUPs with identical wording? Should teachers or students sign AUPs attesting they agree to abide by the policies specified within as a condition to use school-supported technology, or should both groups merely sign that they have read the AUP? Districts and their lawyers cannot agree. No single AUP serves every district's purpose; sample AUPs abound on the World Wide Web, as well as in legal and educational journals.

After implementing comprehensive AUP policies, districts have prospective mechanisms to deal with students or staff who sign AUPs and then misuse the district's technology resources. Districts should also formulate policies to deal with students or employees who refuse to sign the AUP, or with students whose parents refuse to countersign.

Complying with DMCA

Even though courts have not specifically applied the safe harbor provisions of DMCA to K–12 public schools that act as ISPs, school districts should play it safe and comply with DMCA's requirements in order to avoid liability for copyright infringement. This simply means that school districts should adopt and implement a policy of terminating Internet access for any staff or students who repeatedly violate copyright or who interfere in any way with technology protection measures. Additionally, districts should bar hackers from school-sponsored Internet access. Districts should give notice of this policy through AUPs, teacher contracts, and student handbooks; consequences of prohibited activities should be spelled out in the district disciplinary code. Internet access should be a privilege, not a service to which students and staff are entitled, and access can be predicated on appropriate behavior. If Internet use is part of the district's prescribed curriculum, students who refuse to abide by AUP guidelines must be provided with alternative assignments. Inappropriate behavior in the technology setting should have consequences.

> Internet access should be a privilege, not a service to which students and staff are entitled, and access can be predicated on appropriate behavior.

The district should designate an official to whom copyright violations on the district Web site can be reported. A mechanism should be in place for checking reported violations and, if substantiated, for removing violations from the Web site as soon as they become verified. The name of the designated official, a statement that the district encourages reporting of copyright infringements, and the method with which violations will be verified and removed should be clearly visible on the district home page. The district should consider paying the $20 filing fee to list this individual on the Copyright Office Web site.

The district also should adopt guidelines for alerting users of the school Internet service to the issues involved in prolonged local caching. Proxy caching is under district control, and the district webmaster must carefully monitor district caching practices.

The district should centralize control of its main Web site and the sites of individual schools, teachers, students, clubs, and other district representatives. Everything on the district Web site and everything directly connected with the Web site by links should represent the educational mission of the district. The webmaster should carefully scrutinize text for possible typos and educational suitability. Graphics should be in good taste. The webmaster also should work for fair representation of all segments of the district population.

The district should formulate and adopt a policy for uploading student work, especially personally identifiable information and student images, on the Web site. Bear in mind that the potential audience for the Web site is the world, which includes the perverts and child predators in this country and abroad.

Copyright law establishes no minimum age for holding a copyright on original work. The district must respect children's rights, as well as adults' rights.

Annotated Legal References

Information about copyright and compliance is widely available on the Internet, including on the following sites:

- The U.S. Copyright Office maintains two Web sites: http:// lcweb.loc.gov/copyright and http://www.loc.gov/copyright.
- The Copyright Clearance Center (CCC), a licenser for text reproduction rights, contains articles and links to copyright law at www.copyright.com.
- Specific information on copyright law and recent litigation can be found on Cornell Law School's Legal Information Institute Web site at http://www.law.cornell.edu/topics/ copyright.html.

Statutes

- The Copyright Act of 1976 is codified in the U.S. Code at 17 U.S.C. § 501 and following sections.
- The Digital Millennium Copyright Act is Public Law 105-304, passed in 1998.

Court Decisions

Two important cases that illustrate how courts analogize the Internet to more traditional forms of communication and formulate Internet-related copyright decisions are

- *MAI Systems Corporation v. Peak Computer, Inc.*, 991 F.2d 511 (9th Cir. 1993), and
- *Religious Technology Center v. Netcom On-line Communications Services, Inc.*, 907 F. Supp. 1361 (N.D. Cal. 1995).

5

Copyright and the
Internet in Schools

WITH EASY ACCESS TO INFORMATION ON THE INTERNET, TEACHERS AND students are accustomed to using the technology in their own work and research. This ease of access, however, makes copyright infringement in schools much more possible and frequent. Districts need to know how Internet technology can violate copyright and what guidelines they must follow to try to avoid infringement.

Fair Use of Copyrighted Works
by Teachers and Students

Since the mid-1880s, teachers and researchers have relied on an exception to copyright protection called *fair use*. This important part of copyright law supersedes the author's exclusive right to duplicate and distribute his works for public policy reasons, recognizing the tension between an author's ownership rights and society's desire to use his works. Although legal scholars continue to debate whether fair use is a right or a privilege, the distinction is irrelevant to teachers and students. They simply want to use material, especially from the Internet, without needing the author's permission or paying licensing fees and royalties. Section 107 of the Copyright Act of 1976 specifically provides for "fair use" of copyrighted materials for teaching, scholarship, or research, as well as for literary criticism, commentary, news reporting, and parody. Teachers may even make multiple copies for classroom use.

The legal standard for deciding what constitutes fair use of a copyrighted work involves examining and balancing the effects of four different relevant factors:

1. Whether the purpose and character of the use are of a commercial nature or are for nonprofit educational purposes.
2. Whether the nature of the copyrighted work itself is primarily factual or creative.
3. How much of the work is used, or how substantial is the part used, in relation to the copyrighted work as a whole.
4. How the use affects the author's ability to market and realize a profit from the work.

The most important factor in a given case depends on the totality of the circumstances, which presents a difficult analysis in most cases. What is perfectly clear, however, is that the doctrine of fair use is not a blanket permission to use an author's work without permission, even for teachers.

The Fair Use Guidelines

Because applying the fair use factors is so difficult, a group of educators, authors, and publishers authorized by Congress produced guidelines on reproducing books and periodicals for use in not-for-profit educational institutions. Published in 1976 as a supplement to the actual Copyright Act, the "Agreement on Guidelines for Classroom Copying in Not-for-Profit Educational Institutions with Respect to Books and Periodicals" states the minimum standards for permissible copying. Other guidelines followed between 1979 and 1999 for off-air recordings of broadcast programming, digital images, educational multimedia, and distance learning. Although not incorporated into the Copyright Act, they provide school districts with a minimum standard of what constitutes fair use. Districts should be reasonably safe from copyright violations if they follow the guidelines.

The guidelines, like the legal standard described earlier, establish a four-part test for fair use in schools. When copies are made, the copied portion must be

1. Brief,
2. Spontaneous,
3. Limited in cumulative effect, and
4. Affixed with a copyright notice acknowledging proper authorship.

The guidelines describe *brevity* as "a complete article, story or essay of less than 2,500 words," a complete poem of less than 250 words, or "an excerpt from any prose work of not more than 1,000 words or 10 percent of the work." *Spontaneity* means that the teacher's inspired decision to use the work and the actual use must be so close in time that seeking the author's permission to use the work is impossible. The *cumulative effect limitation* means that a teacher can make multiple copies of any given work for only one class in the school. Of course, fair use never justifies unauthorized copying of any parts of consumable workbooks.

Fair Use in Videotaping

The 1979 "Guidelines for Off-Air Recording of Broadcast Programming for Educational Purposes" address videotaping of copyrighted television programs by nonprofit educational institutions. These guidelines allow recording for educational purposes, but prescribe a 45-day limit on institutions' retaining the copies. The tapes must be destroyed or erased at the end of the 45 days, unless the institution obtains a license.

Caching

Caching is a potential copyright violation unique to the Internet. The process of caching involves storing information in a designated space on a computer hard drive or server from which retrieval is fast and easy. Entire Web sites are cacheable at the level of the individual user, who uses a "back" button to retrieve information stored in the computer's RAM (where it is called *local caching*) or at the server level (called *proxy caching*). Although caching by individual users usually involves transitory storage of information, materials saved by proxy caching could purposefully or inadvertently reside on a school server for weeks or even months. Caching may involve potentially serious copyright violations if Web sites supported by advertising are stored for lengthy periods of time, even though DMCA specifically exempts ISPs from liability because of caching activities. When Web developers update their Web sites, caches remain unchanged; cache users could thus receive outdated information. This activity is not necessarily a copyright violation, but it may have disadvantageous consequences in education. If users cache commercial sites, such caches may hurt advertisers whose information on the cache becomes outdated or even completely obsolete. Caches also could deprive Web site creators or owners of accurate information about "hits," or how many times users accessed the site.

If proxy caching is a necessary evil in a school district because of slow Internet access speeds or other technology problems, districts must review cached information periodically and adopt and enforce maximum storage times.

Linking

The ability to *link* sites on the Internet is one of the Net's most educationally innovative features. Links are embedded electronic addresses that direct the user from one Web site to other related sites or from one Web page to another. Links can be one of two types: outlinks, which allow browsers to go from the original site to another one by clicking on a displayed button; or inline links, which bring images, audio clips, or documents to the original site from a different one. This second kind of link is also called *framing*, because the border or text header of the original site remains displayed around the imported Web page. Framing is a potential violation of copyright because it makes one independently created Web site look like part of another.

Although links have the capacity to foster integration and creativity in teaching and learning, linking also has the potential to increase copyright violations because it facilitates movement among sites so rapidly and makes it easy to "cut" and "paste" information from a site to an electronic document. Simply following a link is not a copyright violation, even if the link leads to copyrighted material. Potential liability arises when Internet users take advantage of the ease of accessing information and "forget" that the material they acquire may be copyrighted.

Links may also confuse users about the advertisers or sponsors of a site, especially if only parts of a Web site are incorporated via online links. Web site visitors may incorrectly attribute the content of a link. This may raise trademark issues as well as copyright issues. Linking to the interior pages of a Web site without accessing the home page, called *deep linking*, can raise allegations of trespassing and other property-related offenses, including copyright infringement.

Works for Hire

The tension in copyright between authors' proprietary rights to their creations and the public's right to information and access to creative works presumes that someone can somehow identify the author. Yet who the author is for copyright purposes is not always clear. If a teacher writes a short play for her class to perform, is she the author? Does she become the copyright owner at the moment she fixes the text of the play in tangible form? Or does the school district for whom she works and who pays her salary become the copyright owner? The answer, again, is that "it depends."

The Copyright Act of 1976 includes a provision that defines "works made for hire." According to the law, an employer or other person for whom the work is made is the author and owner of all copyright rights unless the involved parties expressly agreed otherwise in writing before the work's creation. In other words, the employer owns by default the copyright to works made by employees. This stipulation can have important financial consequences—perhaps not for teachers who create short classroom plays, but for teachers who develop publishable workbooks, exam preparation manuals, lesson plans, or visual and sculptural works.

If a signed written agreement between the school board (or designated agent) and the teacher gives sole authorship to the teacher prior to a work's creation, the teacher becomes the author and copyright owner. Even when the creation of the work proceeds in the absence of a written agreement, as is most often the case, the teacher may be able to claim authorship and copyright rights. Who the author is depends on whether the teacher created the work in question within the scope of her employment. That is, did the teacher create the work during normal working hours, with materials supplied by the district, in order to more efficiently or effectively perform her job? If so, the work is a work made for hire, and the copyright and all financial gain accruing from the work belong to the school district.

> Linking also has the potential to increase copyright violations because it facilitates movement among sites so rapidly and makes it easy to "cut" and "paste" information from a site to an electronic document.

On the other hand, if the teacher was not acting as an employee within the scope of her employment when she created the work, and instead was an independent contractor performing the work, the situation may reverse. The independent contractor case requires a written agreement between the teacher and her employer before the district can claim authorship. Moreover, only a limited number of categories of works created by an independent contractor can become works made for hire. These categories, however, include works that teachers may help create outside the scope of their normal employment, including

- Contributions to collective works, such as chapters to books;
- Tests;
- Answer materials for tests;
- Instructional texts;

- Supplementary works to assist in understanding another author's works;
- Compilations; and
- Translations.

If a teacher creates works in these categories and is paid either by a school district that is not employing her or by some other institution or agency, then the teacher is working ("moonlighting" is the slang term) as an independent contractor; she retains authorship and copyright rights over her product, unless she assigns her rights to whoever pays her with a written agreement signed by both parties that indicates the copyright holder.

The line between works made for hire and works created under an independent contractor arrangement gets fuzzy and more complicated when a teacher asserts copyright ownership over a work created spontaneously and without pay. For example, a teacher who creates and markets a potentially successful educational game developed while working as a teacher in District A may want to sell her copyright in the game to a vendor. District A might claim copyright ownership, alleging that the game, even if created at the teacher's home outside classroom hours, is a work of the kind the employee was hired to perform, created within the scope of the teacher's employment. As the line between the home and the traditional workplace blurs, conflicts like this may occur with increasing frequency. At the college and university level, where professors are expected to "publish or perish," the courts have carved out a "teacher exception" to the work-for-hire provision: faculty writings are not works made for hire, and the authors retain copyright ownership even if they use university resources. The courts, however, have not yet explicitly extended this exception to teachers in the K–12 public school setting. The education community, however, has tacitly adopted it in the pre-college setting.

Trademark Infringement

Trademark infringement on the Internet is an issue related to copyright. Trademarks are valuable shortcuts by which a company establishes consumer recognition and elicits goodwill toward its products. Misuse of a company's trademark to confuse the public as to the origin or quality of goods and services is a violation of federal law carrying stiff penalties—civil and criminal. Along with importing a company's trademark to a Web site, using a site's trademarked metatags to attract hits to another site is trademark infringement. Companies that put a high price on consumer goodwill keenly patrol metatag infringement.

Recommendations for Schools

Promulgating the Fair Use Guidelines

Building administrators should provide all teachers in the district with a simple written list of the guidelines for fair use of printed materials, as described previously, and direct that copies be permanently affixed to every copy machine in the building. The guidelines should put teachers on notice that the following activities are strictly prohibited and will result in disciplinary action:

- Indiscriminate copying of materials, whether hard copy or online, even if the material does not bear a copyright notice.
- Copying computer programs, except for archiving or backing up personally owned copies.
- Copying consumables, including workbooks, proprietary worksheets, standardized tests, test booklets, and answer keys, unless specific permission of the publisher is given in writing.
- Copying short articles, essays, or graphics to create anthologies or class collections.
- Copying in excess of the fair use guidelines for print materials.

Teachers may make one copy of any work for personal research or scholarship, or make multiple copies for classroom use, provided that the materials are used for only one class and that the materials comport with the fair use guidelines for print materials. Teachers must put a copyright notice on all copied print materials.

For the special case of printed musical scores, administrators should inform teachers that the fair use guidelines for educational uses of music parallel the guidelines for print materials. Teachers may not copy music to avoid paying for music. Teachers also may not copy material for performances unless authorized copies are unavailable and performance is imminent. Copyright notice must appear on all copied music.

With respect to videotape recordings of television programs, teachers may not repeatedly use the videotape in class. Teachers must show videotapes within 10 days of recording, and they must destroy or erase them within 45 days. Teachers also may not combine tapes to create anthologies, and they must include copyright notice with any recording.

> Misuse of a company's trademark to confuse the public as to the origin or quality of goods and services is a violation of federal law carrying stiff penalties—civil and criminal.

Although no guidelines are in place for multimedia presentations (i.e., presentations using computer images, music, sounds, etc.), teachers should follow the print and off-air broadcast guidelines as general rules.

In face-to-face teaching activities, where teachers and students are in the same classroom (excluding distance learning classes or teleconferences), teachers may perform or display copyrighted dramatic works and have their students perform or display such works, provided copies of those works are lawfully made or obtained. Teachers may use nondramatic literary or musical works more expansively as long as they do not directly or indirectly charge admission to the performances; they may even transmit them if the works are part of systematic instructional activities and are transmitted to places where educational activities take place regularly. For example, music teachers may use copyrighted musical works without permission in order to stage a class concert at school. The school must not profit financially from the performance, however. If the school charges admission, all proceeds from the performance must go directly back to education of students.

The district must constantly remind employees and students that copyright applies to works on the Internet with the same force as to traditional media.

Adopting a Clear Policy of Copyright Ownership

Because ascertaining the identity of the copyright owner can be difficult in cases of teacher-created materials, every district should formulate a clear and simple statement of the rights of creators, for both online and hard copy formats. The district owns the copyright to works that teachers make in the course of their employment, except for teachers' scholarly articles in peer-reviewed journals. Many districts want to encourage staff development, and thus adopt very liberal policies toward copyright ownership. They allow teacher-creators to retain copyright ownership to all original works they produce. This works well, except in cases where teachers begin to reap sizeable profits from their creations, or where teachers begin to neglect traditional duties. Other districts adopt very strict copyright policies, naming the district copyright owner of all teacher work related to the district's educational purpose. This works until teachers feel that the district is taking advantage of them. The best solution is somewhere in the middle, but the middle ground needs to be clearly identified.

Districts have no work-for-hire claim to students' work, because students are not employees of the district. Before uploading or displaying any student work on the Internet, district employees should always obtain students' *and* their parents' written permission, because students are minors in the eyes of the law and unable to give binding consent. Privacy concerns, which are discussed in Chapter 3, also apply.

Deciding the Appropriate Level of Control

The school board must decide, with the assistance of counsel, how strictly they will regulate fair use of copyrighted materials by teachers in the district. The guidelines for fair use set out a strict interpretation of the doctrine; teachers can probably use copyrighted materials more expansively than the guidelines dictate without being liable for copyright infringement. For example, the guidelines specify that a teacher or school librarian must destroy or erase a videotape of a public television broadcast not more than 45 days after its taping. Will teachers or librarians be guilty of copyright infringement if, for pedagogical reasons, they keep the videotape to show two months after its taping date? Probably not. The board has to decide what it wants its policy to accomplish. Copy restrictions placed on teachers may result in a loss of spontaneity in bringing students important information, but a *laissez faire* or neglectful attitude toward teachers' indiscriminate copying of copyrighted materials may result in district liability for copyright infringement.

Annotated Legal References

Information about copyright fair use guidelines is available on several government-sponsored and private Web sites, including the following:

- The U.S. Copyright Office maintains two Web sites: http://lcweb.loc.gov/copyright/ and http://www.loc.gov/copyright/.
- Stanford University also maintains an extensive Web site with fair use information at http://fairuse.stanford.edu.
- Specific information about multimedia fair use guidelines is available at Pennsylvania State University's Web site at http://www.libraries.psu.edu/mtss/fairuse/guidelinedoc.html.

6

E-mail and the School Internet

INTERNET-ENABLED ELECTRONIC MAIL, OR E-MAIL, IS A STAR TREK-LIKE experience. With e-mail, a sender's word-processed message or visual image is "beamed" through cyberspace instantaneously to one or many recipients. Using a *screen name*, a sender becomes anonymous; no handwriting or voiceprint betrays identity. Using the school Internet, students and teachers can communicate in complete privacy . . . or so they may think. In fact, e-mail is not secure unless it is encrypted. Moreover, third parties are legally free to read and make use of whatever e-mail messages arrive at their computer terminals, whether in error or by design.

Privacy in E-mail Communication

The easiest place to start in explaining the privacy rights of e-mail users in the school context is with school district employees who have e-mail access at work. Although courts in several states are grappling with the free speech issues surrounding anonymous Internet postings in chat rooms and on Web sites, the expectation of privacy in employer-sponsored e-mail communications is clearly defined. Put simply, there is none. Even if employees use confidential passwords to access e-mail, and even if employers give assurances that e-mail communications are confidential, the courts have ruled that employers who provide e-mail for business purposes can still monitor their employees' communications.

In 1983, the Supreme Court recognized school districts' rights to reserve the district's internal mail system exclusively for school matters, as long as the district's regulation is reasonable and not an attempt merely to suppress expression with which the district disagrees. School districts that provide e-mail to facilitate school-related communications among teachers and staff can, and do in many cases, access employee communications at will; employees have no expectation of privacy in such district-sponsored e-mail. At least one court has gone even further, ruling that state employees have no expectation of privacy in *any* Internet use at work.

Students, however, are not school employees and, because they do not shed their constitutional rights at the schoolhouse gate, student communications via school-sponsored e-mail may be protected under the First Amendment. Many schools, realizing the potential legal issues, do not support student e-mail use on district computers. Students communicate online by postings to district-maintained and district-supervised public folders. Students may require passwords to access and post messages to such folders, but because district personnel supervise the folder, there are no expectations of privacy in their communications.

Regulating E-mail Communications

Both federal and state statutes regulate e-mail communications. Title I of the federal Electronic Communications Privacy Act (ECPA) of 1986 protects e-mail communications from intentional interception. However, merely reading another's e-mail on a computer screen is not an "interception." Interceptions must occur during the actual course of the transmission in order for Title I of the ECPA to apply.

Title II of ECPA, on the other hand, prohibits unauthorized accessing of stored e-mails. It provides no penalty, however, for private individuals who read someone else's stored e-mails, even if they later disclose the contents to third parties, who then use the information for their own purposes. Title II applies only to disclosure or use of stored e-mails by the provider of the service that transmitted the e-mail.

State laws also apply to e-mail communications, but most mirror ECPA, sharing the same gaps in statutory protections. These gaps have engendered several interesting court cases involving schools. Perhaps the most interesting was a 1999 case in Pennsylvania, where the district accused its own technology coordinator of intercepting and relaying to a school board member 30 e-mail messages from the technology coordinator's supervisor, the assistant superintendent, over a two-month period. The court ruled that the technology coordinator had not intercepted the messages during transmission, because he had simply copied incoming messages to a folder for backup and storage. The court also ruled that the technology coordinator had accessed the stored e-mails in the course of performing his job responsibility to monitor operation of the district's computers. The judge dismissed all charges. The exonerated technology coordinator now directs technology services at a distinguished Pennsylvania university.

Offensive E-mail

Because e-mail is so easy to use and appears to be both secure and anonymous, students and staff members who have access to district e-mail may succumb to the temptation to transmit inappropriate jokes or even more offensive communications. What should a district do if a student uses the school e-mail to transmit tasteless jokes or racial slurs, or to threaten or harass another student or staff member? What if a staff member uses school e-mail inappropriately, including threatening or harassing students, colleagues, or even community members?

School districts face two issues in this regard. Districts must determine if the alleged threat or harassment is actionable under the law and, independently of that determination, districts must decide whether to take disciplinary action against the person creating the offensive e-mail.

Threatening E-mail

To be actionable under the law, a threat must be a *true threat*, a legal term of art defined under federal and state statutes, and interpreted by the courts when deciding whether First Amendment protection applies to the communication.

Courts typically take one of two approaches in deciding whether a statement is a true threat or protected expression. First, they look to see if the person issuing the alleged threat could reasonably foresee that his or her communication would be perceived as a serious intent to harm. Alternatively, some courts look immediately to the recipient of the communication. Would a reasonable person, in light of the surrounding circumstances, interpret the communication as a threat? However the courts begin their inquiry, the standard applied is an objective, not subjective, standard. What would a reasonable person in the circumstances believe?

Courts do not always arrive at what seems to be the "right" answer. For example, a Michigan court dismissed charges against a University of Michigan student who posted graphic, sexually violent stories on an Internet user group site. One of the stories described the torture, rape, and murder of a young woman with the same name as a female classmate of the male student. At about the same time, the student exchanged e-mails with an acquaintance in Ontario, Canada, graphically describing his intent to commit sexually violent acts against women and children. Declining to label the e-mail communications as true threats, the court said that, to be a true threat, the statement must be directly communicated to the threatened individual. The e-mail communication in this case, the court ruled, was not direct enough. The University of Michigan student and his Canadian e-mail correspondent were simply "fostering friendship based on shared sexual fantasies."

Similarly, a Wisconsin court decided that an 8th grade student was not communicating a true threat when he wrote in an in-class creative writing assignment of his intent to kill his teacher. The court drew the distinction between true threats and "hyperbole, jest, innocuous talk, and expressions of political views," adding that before the expression could be considered a true threat, the speaker must have the ability to carry out the threat. The court, however, distinguished between threats punishable under law and offensive student speech punishable under school district discipline codes, and upheld the right of the school to discipline the student.

A federal court in western Pennsylvania used traditional legal principles governing student expression in schools to exonerate a high school student, Zachariah Paul, suspended from school for compiling a "Top Ten" list of insults aimed at the school's athletic director. The student, apparently a well-known creator of such insult lists, did not carry his written list to school because school authorities had warned him of possible punishment. He e-mailed the list to a friend from his home computer. An undisclosed friend, however, reformatted the list and distributed it on school grounds. School administrators then suspended Paul for 10 days.

After summarizing and reviewing the U.S. Supreme Court decisions in *Tinker, Fraser,* and *Kuhlmeier* (see Chapter 1), the court noted that the school district had not demonstrated evidence that "teachers were incapable of teaching or controlling their classes" because of the list's dissemination in school. Also, the court applied the *Fraser* and *Kuhlmeier* standards to the student's allegedly lewd and obscene comments, holding that schools cannot discipline students for speech made outside the academic environment merely because they consider it to be inappropriate.

Content-Neutral Regulations

The First Amendment does not protect "lewd, vulgar, indecent, and plainly offensive" speech in schools. Statements of intent to cause physical harm to a teacher are plainly offensive, and the school, in keeping with its mission to educate, can discipline students who express such statements. However, schools cannot prohibit speech expressed by students or staff simply because school officials disagree with their expressed opinions. Regulation of speech must be content neutral. The same content-neutral standard applies to speech by staff members.

E-mail Harassment

E-mails that do not rise to the level of true threats may still be harassment. The Supreme Court has not squarely addressed whether harassment that is expressed purely in the form of speech without accompanying conduct receives First Amendment protection. E-mail harassment may be as "simple" as *spamming*—the practice of sending repeated, unsolicited e-mail messages to a large audience of potential readers. Recipients cannot control the receipt of such e-mail, and requests to discontinue the mailings either go unheeded or actually exacerbate the problem because respondents' e-mail addresses are shared among other "spammers." Although difficult to control and largely unregulated by legislation, spam e-mail is an annoyance, but it is usually not harassment directed to any specific person.

> The First Amendment does not protect "lewd, vulgar, indecent, and plainly offensive" speech in schools.

Prohibitions of harassment in schools come from several key federal statutes, two of which are especially important in the school e-mail context. State statutes may also prohibit school e-mail harassment, but as in the ECPA context, they largely mirror the federal statutes.

The two federal statutes that school districts should especially note are

- Title VI of the Civil Rights Act of 1964, providing that no person shall be excluded from, denied the benefits of, or subjected to discrimination under any program or activity receiving federal assistance *because of race, color, or national origin*; and
- Title IX of the Education Amendments of 1972, providing that no person shall be excluded from, denied the benefits of, or subjected to discrimination under any program or activity receiving federal assistance *because of sex or gender*.

Students who believe that they are being subjected to harassment that excludes them from federally funded educational opportunities or denies them the benefits of such educational opportunities because of race, color, national origin, or gender can initiate a lawsuit against the harasser. The harasser may be another student or a district employee, like a teacher. If the harasser is a district employee, the student also will assuredly sue the school district. To succeed in holding the district liable, the student must prove that she provided actual notice of the harassment to a school official with the authority to take corrective action, but that the official was deliberately indifferent to the employee's misconduct. What constitutes "actual notice" is frequently litigated, but if the harassment occurs by e-mail, the student may subpoena school records to provide documentation of actual notice, such as a district-maintained log of student and employee e-mail use.

Employees of a school district familiar with their employer's ability to trace and reconstruct technology use are not likely to commit e-mail harassment. However, e-mail may be an attractive vehicle for student-on-student harassment. If a public school student suffers gender-based harassment at the hands of another student, she can sue her harasser and his or her family. Victimized students also have a right under the law to sue the school district for *hostile environment* harassment. Here the student bears an even heavier burden in trying to prove the school district is liable than in proving teacher-student harassment. First, the student must show that she gave actual notice of the harassment to a school official who had the power to correct the situation but was deliberately indifferent to her situation. Secondly, the student must also show that the harassment was so pervasive, severe, and objectively offensive that it deprived her of educational opportunities or benefits that would have otherwise been available in school. This burden is heavy but not insurmountable, and courts have ruled against school districts that disregarded student-on-student harassment. A case of hostile environment harassment by e-mail, however, has not yet appeared in courts.

Cyberstalking

Stalking with e-mail, or *cyberstalking*, is an escalated form of harassment, one that has increased in both schools and the business community in general. That the stalking occurs by e-mail may, perversely, be a boon to the victim, because the recipient can preserve an e-mail log documenting the harassment. The same log may also serve to document that the victim provided actual notice of harassment to school authorities but that the district was deliberately indifferent to the complaints.

> That the stalking occurs by e-mail may, perversely, be a boon to the victim, because the recipient can preserve an e-mail log documenting the harassment.

Overall, e-mail harassment has not been an attention-getting problem for school districts. Perhaps districts have avoided serious e-mail problems because so few districts actually allow unrestricted student access to district e-mail. Student hacking into teachers' e-mail accounts is a greater problem. Districts need to be aware of potential problems, however, when they decide whether to implement student e-mail accounts and respond to allegations of e-mail harassment by students or staff members.

Recommendations for School Districts

The steps a school district should take to ensure it remains safe from liability stemming from e-mails depend on the extent to which the district provides e-mail services. The most manageable situation is that where a school district limits e-mail communication within and through a district intranet.

In this arrangement, users connecting to the internet and their e-mail accounts from within the district must log on to the district server with their user names and passwords. Accessing district e-mail from outside the district is possible, but the path of connection is usually through the district Web site, and access requires a recognizable user name and password. District servers do not support communications routed through commercial Internet service providers (ISPs), like America Online, Prodigy, or Microsoft Net. Those accessing e-mail through the district server can send and receive e-mail from outside users as well as from district people; however, the server does not enable communicating through e-mail link within Internet Web sites. All e-mail contacts must originate through the district interface.

In this very manageable scenario, the school district can put a disclaimer at the entrance portal to the Intranet, requiring would-be users to agree to use district computer resources and facilities solely for educational purposes. The portal screen also can warn that all uses and communications supported by the district are subject to supervision and control, and that no expectation of privacy exists in any expression enabled or supported by the district. If all users under this scenario are district employees, the district has a legally recognized right to limit employee communications to business purposes and, concomitantly, the right to supervise employees' communications. This is the easy case.

Adding to the School E-mail Community

Management of e-mail communications gets progressively more complicated as the community of individuals who have access to district-supported e-mail grows. Students, for example, are not employees. Neither are school board members, district volunteer helpers, independent contractors, or any of other people to whom the district might consider extending district-supported e-mail access. The district's legal mandate to impose conditions on non-employees before granting e-mail access can differ depending on the applicants' relationship to the district. The most manageable scenario is still to provide access to all nonemployee groups through the district server or local network.

Students and E-mail Access

Student access to e-mail is a privilege, not a right, unless such access is necessary to participate in educational programs approved by the district. Even then, the district can assert the right to supervise and monitor student e-mail communications originating in the school context or supported by the district.

Student supervision is, after all, the school's responsibility. The district should put students on notice that they have no expectation of privacy in school-supported e-mail communications. The district should also notify students that it will not tolerate the initiation, forwarding, or saving of inappropriate or noneducational communications on district computers. In setting out the parameters of what constitutes inappropriate student e-mail, however, the district must be careful to say enough, but not too much.

The First Amendment AGAIN . . . .

Districts must exercise discretion in seeking to limit student speech, even on district-owned computers and in district-sponsored e-mail. The legal standard is that school districts can suppress student speech or expression only when the effect of that speech materially disrupts school operations or interferes with the rights of other students to obtain an education. "Undifferentiated fear of disturbance or apprehension of disturbance" is not enough to justify school officials' suppressing student speech. The threat of disturbance must be specific, immediate, and substantial. This standard applies to student e-mails as well.

With potentially harassing student e-mail communications, the situation is the same: school districts must be careful to say enough, but not too much. Threats of physical violence do not receive First Amendment protection. School officials can and should deal with true threats quickly and decisively, invoking both the legal system as well as the school disciplinary code. With potential student e-mail harassment, however, school officials must be careful to distinguish between harassment that is statutorily prohibited and mere expression of disagreeable student opinions. Insulting comments directed toward a student in person or in an e-mail without causing a systemic denial of participation in the educational program may not be the kind of student-student interaction the district has a statutory mandate to regulate. The insults or harassing speech must threaten to deny a victim participation in programs because of race, color, national origin, or gender before the district has the right and duty to regulate such expression. Districts must expend the greatest care when crafting regulations that restrict student expression, and they should seek the advice of legal counsel.

School board members, district volunteer helpers, independent contractors, or any other individuals who access school-supported e-mail can be notified of their rights and responsibilities by requiring that they access their e-mail accounts through the district server with its carefully worded provisos for would-be users. Because access to and use of the district e-mail system is a mutually voluntary arrangement, districts have the right to determine the conditions governing participation in the system, subject to the same First Amendment concerns expressed above.

Unregulated E-mail Access

Districts that allow unregulated e-mail access through school computers are asking for trouble. Establishing district-supported e-mail accounts through commercial ISPs puts districts at the mercy of those services' regulatory and supervisory policies. Although some ISPs have adopted responsible and legally defensible e-mail user policies, there are no guarantees that these policies will suit the needs of any given school district. The ability to establish user profiles that some ISPs provide could create student privacy issues if students provided too much or false information in their profile. Districts should retain control over their e-mail systems by limiting access through their own servers. If such centralized control does not accommodate all the potential users, districts should limit e-mail access to the types of district stakeholders that the servers can accommodate. Potential users whom the district server cannot accommodate because of storage limitations or connection speeds—students perhaps— should be required to use district-maintained public folders for posting and responding to communications. If a district decides to use such public folders, it must carefully examine its options and responsibilities under the Family Educational Rights and Privacy

> With potential student e-mail harassment, however, school officials must be careful to distinguish between harassment that is statutorily prohibited and mere expression of disagreeable student opinions.

Act, or FERPA. (See the discussion of district responsibilities under FERPA in Chapter 3.)

The Special Role of the District's Network Administrator

The key role of the school district's network administrator in overseeing the e-mail system deserves emphasis. The network administrator must be knowledgeable in all aspects of system coordination and supervision, sensitive to legal issues, and willing to collaborate with the district's legal counsel when appropriate. The network administrator plays a critical role in establishing and enforcing policies for maintaining district e-mail logs and allocating storage space on the district server for all aspects of network e-mail documentation. Districts should expect to compete with the private sector for such expertise.

Annotated Legal References

Statutes

- The federal statute criminalizing interstate communications containing true threats is 18 U.S.C. § 875, current through Public Law 107-89, approved December 18, 2001.
- Title VI of the Civil Rights Act of 1964 can be found at 42 U.S.C. § 2000.
- Title IX of the Education Amendments of 1972 can be found at 20 U.S.C. § 1681.
- The Electronic Communications Privacy Act of 1986 can be found at 18 U.S.C. § 2511.

Court Decisions

- Threats of physical violence are not protected under the First Amendment. See *Watts v. United States*, 394 U.S. 705 (1969).
- The Supreme Court ruled that school districts have the right to reserve the public school's internal mail system for district

purposes, as long as they adopt reasonable regulations and do not attempt to suppress expression merely because they disagree with the speakers' views. See *Perry Education Association v. Perry Local Educators' Association*, 460 U.S. 37 (1983).

- The Supreme Court found a private right of action under Title IX to redress teacher-to-student harassment based on gender in *Franklin v. Gwinnett County Public Schools*, 503 U.S. 60 (1992), and set out the parameters of the plaintiff's burden of proof six years later in *Gebser v. Lago Vista Independent School District*, 524 U.S. 274 (1998). A year later the Court wrestled with the issue of student-on-student sexual harassment in *Davis v. Monroe County Board of Education*, 526 U.S. 1629 (1999), establishing the parameters of the private right of action for hostile environment harassment.

- Courts have ruled that employers can monitor employees' e-mail communications, even if employers provide confidential passwords to access e-mail and even if employers give assurances that e-mail communications are confidential. See *Smyth v. Pillsbury Company*, 914 F. Supp. 97 (E.D. Pa. 1996), *Bourke v. Nissan Motor Corporation*, No. B068705 (Cal. Ct. App. July 26, 1993) (unreported decision), available at http://www.loudy.com/CASES/Bourke_v_Nissan.html, and *McLaren v. Microsoft Corporation*, 1999 WL 339015 (Tex. App. Dallas).

- The e-mail case involving the University of Michigan student was *United States v. Baker*, 890 F. Supp. 1375 (E.D. Mich. 1995). Jake Baker's real name was Abraham Jacob Alkabaz. On appeal the Sixth Circuit upheld the Michigan decision in *United States v. Alkabaz*, 104 F.3d 1492 (6th Cir. 1997). A petition for rehearing and a suggestion for rehearing *en banc* (by all the Circuit Judges sitting together) were both denied later that same year.

- Several courts have ruled that there is no expectation of privacy in e-mail communications. See, for example, *United States v. Charbonneau*, 979 F. Supp. 1177 (S.D. Ohio 1997).

- The Pennsylvania case involving alleged e-mail interception by the district's technology coordinator was *Commonwealth v. Friedman*, 47 Chester County Reporter 174 (1999).
- The Wisconsin decision declining to consider the 8th grader's creative writing assignment a true threat to his teacher was *In re: Douglas D.*, 626 N.W.2d 725 (Wis. 2001).
- The western Pennsylvania case involving Zachariah Paul was *Killion v. Franklin Regional School District*, 136 F. Supp.2d 446 (W.D. Pa. 2001).

7

Where Do We Go from Here?

SCHOOL DISTRICTS HAVE A BIG JOB AHEAD OF THEM IN WRESTLING WITH school-related Internet issues. School administrators must take care not to become overly zealous when formulating policies for regulating Internet expression. Just as districts are discovering that applying "zero tolerance" policies on weapons is not appropriate in all cases, adopting and implementing overly strict regulatory policies in regard to Internet expression may not solve technology-related problems in schools. Furthermore, such policies may expose districts to liability for compromising First Amendment protections.

Weighing In on the "More Is Less" Issue

The Third Circuit Court of Appeals in Pennsylvania recently took a public school district to task over a harassment policy it said was too broad. The court distinguished between harassing conduct of a physical kind, which the Constitution does not protect, and harassing speech or expressive conduct, which the First Amendment does protect, even if society finds the expressed views unpleasant and distasteful. The district's policy prohibited harassment on account of sex, race or color, religion, disability, or "other" personal characteristics. The policy applied universally to

conduct by any member of the school community, even to the
school board, school bus drivers, and school visitors.

The plaintiffs who challenged the district policy were ardent
Christians who believed that the policy prevented them from
speaking out about their religious beliefs against homosexuality.
They feared that the district would use the policy to prohibit them
from distributing antigay literature or from engaging in symbolic
activities intended to disseminate their message. The court agreed
with the plaintiffs that the policy was too far-reaching. The problem, the court said, was that the policy impermissibly restricted
harassment based on characteristics not enumerated and protected under federal statutes or constitutional amendments.
Various federal laws, including Title IX, and the Fourteenth
Amendment prohibit discrimination or harassment based on sex,
race, color, national origin, age, or disability. Nothing in the law
prohibits harassment based on "other" characteristics, that is,
characteristics other than those enumerated. Attempting to regulate students' conduct pertaining to their peers' appearance, clothing, or social skills may be "brave, futile, or merely silly," the court
said, but attempting to regulate speech about moral values strikes
at the core of the First Amendment.

Remembering *Tinker, Fraser,* and *Kuhlmeier*

Even in the school setting, where the school is responsible for
teaching socially acceptable behavior and inculcating good citi-
zenship, school officials can regulate students' speech only if it
interferes with the district's educational mission or infringes the
rights of other students to obtain an education. Just because
school administrators think or fear that such interference may
occur is not justification; significant undesirable effects must be
specific and imminent. A previous or concurrent history of racial
unrest in the school may justify punishing a student for drawing
the Confederate flag in class. The drawing may threaten to inflame
student emotions already near the flashpoint. Conversely, at least
one court has taken a school district to task for prohibiting stu-

dents from wearing Confederate flag T-shirts. The school had had no racial problems and had no expectation of disturbance from the students' choice of clothing. Reprising *Tinker*, the court refused to allow an undifferentiated and unfounded fear of disturbance to justify restricting students' expressive conduct.

When crafting school or district policies that regulate students' online speech, school administrators must track the language of applicable statutes, paying particular attention to avoid overstating the regulation. The text of any policies regulating student speech or expressive conduct should not include catch-all phrases like "all," "all other," or "other characteristics." Districts need legal counsel who can inform them about applicable statutes and update them on current regulations, but they also need legal "wordsmiths" who can review policies for vague and overbroad wording.

Protecting Opinions and Values

Student opinions are protected expression, unless expression of the opinions would cause real, documentable, and imminent disruption of the school's operations, or significantly interfere with other students' rights. Student speech about moral values, students' personal values, or the values of others is also protected under the First Amendment. First Amendment protections apply both online and offline. Lewd, vulgar, or profane student speech, however, is not protected expression in the school setting. Schools have the right to regulate such speech precisely because it is lewd, vulgar, or profane. They need not prove that such inappropriate speech disrupted the school's operations.

Schools also may regulate student expression that reasonable observers would view as representing the views of the school or bearing the school's *imprimatur*. Schools can and should preview, monitor, and regulate students' online expression that either appears on the school or district Web site or represents itself to be expression sanctioned by the school.

Involving Parents

Districts should consider formulating and adopting proactive policies that involve parents in helping encourage appropriate online student expression. Part of the process should involve parents setting the example of good online communication. A teacher can model good practices in school, but if a student has home Internet access to the worst that the Web has to offer, the teacher's example can easily be overwhelmed or undone.

> Part of the process should involve parents setting the example of good online communication.

Schools should consider providing information for parents about how to help students find child-friendly Web sites, to recognize and delete spam and other inappropriate e-mail communications, and to protect themselves from child predators or sexual voyeurs. Students involved in the creation and maintenance of inappropriate school-related Web sites often have parental help, even for the most egregiously offensive sites. Parents who assist their teenagers (most frequently the students are young teenagers of middle school age) in creating Web sites that demean their schools, insult their teachers or principals, and "talk trash" about their classmates must be very bitter and unhappy individuals. They certainly seem to have no respect for the public school system or its teachers and administrators. How can the school make a meaningful connection with these parents?

Schools can try to involve parents in setting appropriate expectations for students' Internet use by sending them periodic letters suggesting how they can help. No guarantee accompanies this exhortation. However, the postage costs seem a small price to pay for the potential benefits, even if the immediate results are limited.

Continuing Contacts

The school's first contact with parents in relation to Internet matters will likely be a consent letter and Acceptable Use Policy (AUP) agreement regarding their child's Internet use in school.

Instead of requiring that the parents simply indicate that they read the policy and give their permission, a school might also ask parents to enforce similar rules for *home computer use* by supervising their child's home Internet use.

The AUP mailing could also include a short, separate, one-page explanation for parents of how to block or filter inappropriate Internet content using parental controls, which are available free of charge with most recent World Wide Web interfaces. The mailing should also include Web site addresses for more information, such as the Safe Kids Web Site at www.safekids.com/kidsrules.htm, which gives a list of rules to help children avoid child predators.

A follow-up letter to parents at mid-year could ostensibly update them on school computer use or the district technology services in general, but its main purpose should be to continue the thread of communication with parents. Teachers might also distribute the follow-up letter at parent conferences, especially if parent turnout is consistently high. The letter could list addresses of additional helpful or exemplary Web sites, remind parents of the AUP they signed, and reiterate the portions of the school disciplinary code that spell out the consequences of students' Internet misuse. If teachers are involved in eliciting parental collaboration, they might suggest the addresses of free curriculum-related "Web Quests" that parents and students together would enjoy exploring online. The more time students spend online with a parent accessing fun and educational Web sites, the less time they have to encounter inappropriate and possibly dangerous materials.

School districts have a big job to do in educating students. Increasingly, schools are finding that educating parents is also part of their job. The burgeoning of Internet accessibility and use in K–12 public schools is bringing both messages home very strongly.

What the Future May Hold

Even the most astute futurists seldom get it right. The amazing rate of growth in information technology during the last decade, the increasing dependence of the American people on technology, and the plummeting price tags for sophisticated and miniaturized technological wonders promise to confound contemporary prognosticators. Children in the primary grades can now access more information more quickly than an experienced university librarian could less than a generation ago. Will technology, especially the Internet, bring education to a higher plane in the 21st century? Will students be able to truly comprehend and appreciate the information available on the Internet?

The Promise of Data Management and Interactivity

Administrative software packages and memory-intensive hardware promise to simplify data management and centralize school district records. Distance learning connectivity allows staff development to take place at separate buildings in the district and from a centralized office or university center. Community accessibility to district, school, and teacher Web sites promises improved communications between district officials, teachers, and parents. Parents can read homework assignments online and hold children accountable. Students absent because of illness can keep abreast of class activities online. Poor readers can improve with e-books. Students can stop struggling with overloaded backpacks and carry textbooks on CD-ROMs. All this is possible, but not yet a widespread reality.

Paying for Progress: District Technology Fees

The "digital divide" may turn out to be the actual reality on which the future of American education hinges. Not only do hardware and software purchases cost money, but so do equipment maintenance, consumable supplies like paper and printing cartridges, telephone charges, and even subscription services to educationally worthwhile Internet programs like Connected Classroom and various student online projects. If school districts cannot pay for technology, they cannot take advantage of its great promise. But the fact is that many large urban school districts cannot even pay for traditional supplies, or they allocate funding so haphazardly that distribution of resources is inadequate, inefficient, and ineffective.

To help cover costs, several public school districts have levied miscellaneous technology fees for services traditionally provided free to students. *eSchool News online* reported in September 2001 that one school district in Jefferson County, Colorado, began charging elementary and secondary students technology fees of $5 and $10 per year, respectively, and that a school district in Naperville, Illinois, charges $29 per year for students in grades 1–12. Kindergartners pay half because they attend school only half the day. Educators are divided about the propriety of these charges, and the courts have not considered their legality.

Commercialism on the Web

One of the most annoying features of the World Wide Web, the constant presence of advertising, may also become one of its most problematic features in the educational context. Just as schools wrestled with the advertising of R-rated movies on Christopher Whittle's Channel One, they may have similar issues with Web advertising. The control exercised by commercial entities on the Web, however, is not solely the problem of the educational community. Web domination by megacorporations threatens the very fabric of unfettered communication symbolized by the Internet. Technology giants like Microsoft threaten to put small-scale HTML programmers out of business. The government so far has been an ineffective watchdog.

Authenticating Information

Teaching students to search out and authenticate information found on the Web is imperative, and the task must not be left to beleaguered English or language arts teachers. Just as the concept of writing across the curriculum has gained legitimacy, so must authenticating information become a cross-curricular priority. Primary source material abounds on the Internet and the Web, but so does quackery. Students must realize that anyone can publish a Web page, and slick and clever graphics do not substitute for scholarship. Teachers must know how to guide students in effectively searching for reliable information. They also must teach students how to correctly and completely attribute materials located on the Internet or Web.

Cyberschools and Socialization

Cyberschools are becoming the wave of the future in some states. Pressured by rising enrollments and inadequate physical facilities, school districts in population hotspots like central Florida are turning to online instruction, with teachers reaching out to students sitting at home in their sneakers and sweatpants. Like home schooling, computer-based instruction has commendable features for some children. Part-time computer-based instruction may be appropriate for enrichment or advanced learning experiences for academically gifted students, and full-time, home computer-based instruction sometimes may be appropriate placement for an emotionally or behaviorally compromised student. But will two-dimensional social interaction via computer screen encourage children's social and emotional development and growth? What will American society be like when children no longer remember how to play outside in the sun, or when they fear to leave home because the computer screen is their reality?

Maybe the Internet in schools will usher in a new society, one where technology brings all people together and makes them kinder and gentler, and incredibly more intelligent. Many schools today, however, encourage the use of computers in education simply because they represent technology, and the public believes that technology in education is "good."

Technology Alone Is Not the Answer

A computer is not "technology," and Internet access is not the savior of education. In many cases, student- and teacher-prepared PowerPoint presentations are just colored substitutes for overhead projector presentations. Technology can facilitate unique and motivational learning environments, but only if educators have unique and motivational pedagogical skills. The best use of technology occurs in classrooms where teachers would be effective without it.

Internet access and technology will never be a substitute for experimental explorations in science, but linking investigators through the Internet can add a collaborative dimension that broadens and enriches students' experiences. Data collection by remote probes can prevent drudgery and expand opportunities for meaningful analysis of data and its implications. Communicating in distance-learning programs can bring experiences to rural schools that would otherwise be unattainable. Virtual field trips, tracking global expeditions, online school partnerships—these are all educationally appropriate if managed by a teacher with imagination and a sense of personal adventure. Without that teacher, these innovations are just another public-broadcasting-type television show.

Hand-Held Devices

One of the most potentially frightening technology tools is the hand-held device, such as the PalmPilot or similar devices. Will well-meaning administrators require that each teacher carry one throughout the teaching day, using delicate styluses to input minute-by-minute letter grades for student behaviors? Will administrators sit in classrooms evaluating teachers by pecking numbers on a little screen? Will teachers and administrators sit at faculty meetings pecking out their grocery lists? Will everyone be so attuned to accountability and organization that all spontaneity and fun are lost from education?

> Technology can facilitate unique and motivational learning environments, but only if educators have unique and motivational pedagogical skills.

*   *   *

As the world waits for the new society promised by computers and the Internet, school districts must continue to support exemplary teachers, with or without technology. Computers and the Internet are not a substitute for teaching, learning, and interacting with others. Administrators and teachers alike need to work hard to ensure that technology helps rather than hinders our educational efforts. If they are to succeed, school leaders must also become technology leaders. They must understand the issues and laws arising from technology use and revise district practices and policies accordingly. Schools will continue to be a closely watched arena for legal issues involving new technologies. Educators must rise to the challenge. Technology in K–12 schools must become *teachnology*.

Annotated Legal References

Court Decisions
- The two Confederate flag cases were *West v. Derby Unified School District No. 260*, 206 F.3d 1258 (2000) (where the court upheld the action of the school board in suspending a middle school student who drew a Confederate flag in mathematics class), and *Castorina v. Madison County School Board*, 246 F.3d 536 (6th Cir. 2001) (where, noting the absence of well-founded expectation of disturbance, the court upheld the right of high school students to wear T-shirts depicting the Confederate flag).
- The case dealing with the school district's antiharassment policy was *Saxe v. State College Area School District*, 240 F.3d 200 (3d Cir. 2001) (where the court decided that a school district policy prohibiting harassment was constitutionally overbroad and impermissibly restricted expression protected by the First Amendment).

Formulating Acceptable Use Policies

INTERNET USER AGREEMENTS OR ACCEPTABLE USE POLICIES (AUPs) are essential strategies that allow school districts to notify technology users of expected behavior and set forth the consequences of misuse. Districts should

- Formulate AUPs.
- Promulgate AUPs in draft form.
- Hold meetings where parents and community members can comment on AUP provisions.
- Offer AUPs for formal school board approval.
- Incorporate the AUPs into the district policy manual.

Each AUP should include a signature line for the anticipated user of district technology equipment and services, accompanied by a parent signature line if the user is a child. School districts must decide on one of three approaches to the AUP's wording:

1. Teachers and students sign AUPs with identical wording;
2. Teachers and students sign AUPs attesting that they agree to abide by the policies specified as a condition of using school-supported technology; or
3. Teachers and students merely sign that they have read the AUP.

In addition to teachers and students, nonteaching district employees may have access to technology as part of their job description. Whether the district chooses to require all technology users to sign an AUP, and whether the wording of the AUPs should be uniform for different kinds of users, will depend on the different types and levels of technological access that various groups of users have in the district. The specific technology tasks performed by district personnel also will determine what provisions their AUP should contain.

AUPs for Teachers

If the district requires teachers to sign a district policy agreement as a condition of their employment, and if the school board adopts a district or teacher-specific AUP as policy, districts can safely require teachers to merely sign that they have read and understood the AUP. If AUPs are part of district policy, districts can hold teachers accountable for complying with the AUP policy as a condition of their employment.

AUPs and Students

Nonemployee students stand in a different legal relationship to the district. For maximum self-protection, districts should require all students to sign that they have read the AUP, they understand, and they *agree to abide by* the provisions of the AUP. For student AUPs, an explicit statement in the document should reference the district's student code of conduct, making a violation of the AUP a violation of the code.

Districts also should require parents' permission before giving students in-school Internet access. Districts should require parents to countersign their children's AUP agreements.

What AUPs Should Contain

AUPs should be short and concise—no more than two or three pages in length—so readers do not get lost in the details. Use simple declarative sentences written in the active voice. Include bulleted lists of allowed or prohibited behaviors, formatted into two columns, if necessary, to compact the document.

The AUP should include a brief statement that all Internet materials are protected by copyright unless they are government documents or unless they explicitly grant permission to copy freely. A corollary statement that copying any original material without attribution is plagiarism should accompany the copyright caution.

The AUP also should reference a school board policy that sets out general guidelines for students' and teachers' personal and school-related Web sites (see Appendix C). At a *minimum*, AUPs should state the following expectations:

- District computing facilities will be used exclusively for educational purposes.
- Students and teachers will use educationally appropriate speech and expression when using the Internet and other technological tools.
- Users are responsible for avoiding copyright violations.
- Users have *no* reasonable expectation of privacy in any or all uses of district technology resources.
- Misuse or misappropriation of district technology equipment or services will result in consequences as prescribed by the district's student code of conduct, teachers' collective bargaining agreement, or some other district-adopted disciplinary code, as appropriate.

District technology users should be put on notice that the consequences for misusing technology equipment or services will depend on the nature of the misuse and the degree of substantial and material disruption of the educational process it causes. Users should also know that any disciplinary action employs an escalating scale of penalties, depending on whether the offense is the first, second, and so on. Consequences for student misuse of district technology resources should begin with loss of student privileges, with suspension and expulsion proceedings reserved for the most serious repeat offenders. Consequences for employee violations should follow the collective bargaining steps for discipline where appropriate.

The general AUP guidelines should be expanded in language readily comprehensible to students and teachers, including specific examples of the speech, expression, and conduct proscribed. A nonexhaustive list of examples of prohibited behaviors may include

- Accessing educationally inappropriate Internet materials;
- Using the Internet or school district e-mail for noneducational purposes;
- Tampering with computer operating systems;
- Hacking into district programs;
- Violating the integrity of district servers;
- Unauthorized copying of copyrighted material;
- Plagiarizing;
- Sending or forwarding inappropriate, vulgar, indecent, or harassing e-mail;
- Caching or linking in violation of copyright; and
- Posting personally identifiable information about self, peers, or district personnel to school-related Web sites.

If AUPs include such examples, the documents also should contain a prominent disclaimer stating that the list of prohibited behaviors is *not exhaustive* and is offered for *illustrative purposes only*. All terms mentioned in the AUP, such as "vulgar," "indecent," and "harassing," should be carefully and specifically defined, with reference to an appended glossary.

AUPs and E-mail

Because of statutory gaps in federal privacy protection and the district's right as employer to monitor and intercept district-supported e-mail communications, AUPs should explicitly notify all users that there is no expectation of privacy in e-mail communications provided or supported by the district (e-mail issues are discussed in detail in Chapter 6).

AUPs and School-Related Photographs and Other Information

Districts should also formulate and include in their AUPs policies regarding the display of student and teacher photographs, as well as information about school activities, on school or district Web sites. The AUP should reference separate district guidelines for students' and teachers' personal and school-related Web sites.

Linking to and from the District Web Site

Districts must control links from the district Web site to other sites. Linking into the "middle pages" of another creator's Web site may constitute a copyright violation. Although the law is as yet unsettled, at least one serious allegation of copyright violations by this so-called "hyperlinking" or "deep linking" has been settled out of court. The parties involved in the first deep-linking lawsuit in 1997, Microsoft and Ticketmaster, reached the settlement after protracted legal expenses. For more information about the Ticketmaster suit, see http://www.cli.org/DPost/Linking.html. Linking controversies are international. See http://www. uni-tuebingen.de/.

Although districts cannot prevent other parties from linking to *them*, they should be aware that it is possible for other Web designers to import material from the district Web site and make it appear within an outside border or *frame* that misleads the viewer as to its origin. Framing of this sort is also a copyright violation (copyright is discussed at greater length in Chapters 4 and 5).

Special Employee Privileges

School districts with a predominantly computer-illiterate staff may consider temporarily sanctioning limited personal Internet and e-mail use during nonworking hours as a means of encouraging technological literacy. Staff members can be encouraged to increase computer skills if they see potential personal advantages. This temporary permission, however, must carefully carve out what is permissible personal use and inform staff exactly when they can use district technology resources for personal pursuits. For example, the district may designate special computers in the library for personal staff use. Districts must notify staff that vulgar, obscene, harassing, or other objectionable communications are prohibited. Also, a proxy server filter should be kept in place to make certain that obscene sites are inaccessible even for personal use.

Timeliness of AUPs

Districts should require that students, parents, and staff members sign AUPs annually. Students who transfer to the district also should sign AUPs as part of registration. Districts should centrally file and maintain AUP forms in the office of the district director of technology or the superintendent's designee.

Refusals to Sign AUPs

The district should unequivocally and steadfastly deny access to district-supported equipment and services to any member of the school community who refuses to sign the AUP. With comprehensive AUP policies in place, districts have prospective mechanisms to deal with students or staff who sign the documents and then misuse the district's technology resources. Without signed AUPs, notice to users of expected behaviors and the resulting consequences of misbehavior is lacking. Without notice, discipline is unenforceable. However, districts also should formulate policies to deal with students or employees who refuse to sign the AUP, or with students whose parents refuse to countersign.

Districts should provide school librarians and teachers the names of all students who refuse to sign AUPs or whose parents refuse to countersign. Districts should steadfastly deny technology privileges to these students. Districts should likewise deny access to district technology resources to employees who refuse to sign AUPs, unless special extenuating circumstances apply; districts should have a process to discuss and deliberate such circumstances when they arise. The district may be responsible for providing alternative educational experiences for students without a current and valid AUP, or for offering alternative employment to employees with extenuating circumstances that prevent them from signing. Such circumstances will be rare, and may be subject to legal challenges. Courts have not yet dealt with such issues.

Complying with the Children's Internet Protection Act (CIPA)

Filtering and Blocking Internet Content

Both knowledgeable Internet users and technology specialists can accomplish varying degrees of filtering and blocking of offensive Internet content by employing different programs that interfere with Internet transmissions at different points along their path.

Packet Level Filtering

Packet level filtering or blocking is a sophisticated mechanism that requires programming router computers to compare the Internet protocol (IP) address of the packet sender with a predetermined "black list." Packet level blocking occurs at points where access providers link to the global Internet. Such blocking does not discriminate based on content but makes entire Web sites unavailable based simply on the sender's Internet identity.

Application Level Filtering

Application level blocking or filtering, on the other hand, blocks reception of specific Uniform Resource Locators (URLs). Application level blocking forces users to access the Internet via proxy servers, which compare what users attempt to access with a black list of Web site URLs or similar Internet addresses. Many school districts and libraries interpose proxy servers between technology users and the Internet. These servers may adversely affect some computer applications and slow down some computer operations. Moreover, proxy server-enabled filtering or blocking is not foolproof.

Filtering Software

Over 144 different software filtering programs are available to use on either school and library servers or home computers, most at minimal to no cost. Some of the better-known titles include Bess, CyberSnoop, Net Nanny, Surfwatch, X-STOP, and Yahooligans. These programs filter or block Internet content based on URLs, keywords, or, in some cases, actual human review of Web pages.

A major criticism of most software filtering programs is that they are overbroad, filtering certain words regardless of their context. For example, a program that attempts to prevent students from accessing sexually explicit content might filter Internet sites containing the keyword "breast." *Context sensitive* filtering programs attempt to refine such filtering by examining the context in which the keyword occurs. For a word like "breast," context sensitive filtering would block access to "female breast" but not to "chicken breast." Many software publishers, however, refuse to reveal the keywords they block, so the user cannot ascertain why some perfectly innocent Web sites are inaccessible.

PICS Ratings

Some software filters also use *PICS ratings*—keywords voluntarily used by commercial Web sites through the Platform for Internet Content Selection (PICS) program. Web publishers who voluntarily subscribe to PICS attach keyword labels to their sites, like "nudity," "violence," or "sex," that provide a common format for filtering. Users of certain Web browsers like Microsoft's Internet Explorer have easy access to PICS-formatted ratings. PICS-based labeling services have rated over 300,000 sites around the world.

Filtering Pictures, Too

Sexually explicit material is available on the Internet and World Wide Web in the form of pictures and video as well as text in English and in other world languages. Currently available blocking and filtering software, as described previously, is primarily text-based, screening for sexually suggestive words or known sexually explicit sites by keywords. Text-based screening does not work well for graphics, but screening programs for sexually explicit images are available. For example, Eyeguard software guarantees that users will not be able to view explicit sexual images. The software employs "an advanced image detection engine" that scans information about the access privileges of the user, along with a thumbnail of the offending image. User- or category-specific passwords enable the assignment of different levels of filtering for multiple users of the same computer or network.

Credit Cards and Passwords

Web site operators also can control access to their Web sites by requiring credit card numbers or passwords, but both schemes limit adults' access as well as children's, and neither completely guarantees against cheaters.

No Perfect System

No filtering and blocking system is perfect. Software packages designed to filter sexually explicit content guarantee that they prevent the display of "most" sexually explicit material. *Consumer Reports* magazine recently reported that popular blocking and filtering software failed to block from 18 to 37 percent of sites they judged to be inappropriate for children. One program, Net Nanny, blocked none of the objectionable sites they identified.

Despite the assurances of filtering advocates that only "one in a million" sites is misblocked, any blocking or filtering software presently available is subject to criticism that it is both over- and underinclusive. Moreover, a conservative estimate of the rate of growth of the World Wide Web estimates 2,000,000 new pages added each day, with the average life of a Web page at 75 days. Even if a software package filters Internet content flawlessly when first engineered, it rapidly becomes obsolete. No software manufacturer has the resources to prevent its programs from becoming over- or underinclusive over time.

Complying with CIPA Requirements

On April 5, 2001, the Federal Communications Commission (FCC) released regulations for CIPA compliance for school districts and libraries receiving federal technology funds. The effective date for certifying compliance was October 27, 2001; however, the U.S. Justice Department did not require library compliance under the Library Service and Technology Act until July 31, 2002.

Undertaking Action

Any school or library that receives discounted rates for Internet access, Internet service, or internal connections under the e-rate program must comply with CIPA. The CIPA obligations kick in for funds received after July 1, 2001, and schools will not receive funding unless they began "undertaking action" to certify compliance before CIPA's effective date in July 2002. Undertaking action means that they have taken recorded steps toward complying with CIPA's requirements. For example, the school could present a school board meeting agenda with CIPA compliance as a topic. (Some schools, however, will qualify for a one-year, one-time compliance extension.)

The FCC requires that schools and libraries indicate on Form 486 whether they are compliant, undertaking action, or exempt from CIPA. State Internet networks and consortia must collect the forms from their members and file with the FCC.

The Public Meeting Requirement

CIPA also requires schools and libraries receiving e-rate discounts to hold a public meeting to discuss the entity's Internet safety policy or AUP. The CIPA-compliant Internet safety policy or AUP must address the following elements:

- Access by minors to inappropriate Internet materials.
- Minors' safety when using direct electronic communications like e-mail, chat rooms, and instantaneous message services.
- Hacking and other unauthorized access and unlawful activities by minors online.

- Unauthorized use and dissemination of personally identifiable information regarding minors.
- Minors' access to "harmful" Internet materials.
- A plan to monitor minors' Internet use in schools.

CIPA requires that the plan to monitor minors' Internet use must include the use of "technology protection measures" to prevent children under the age of 17 from accessing visual depictions that are "harmful to minors," are obscene, or are child pornography. The plan must also employ technology protection measures to prevent adults from accessing visual depictions that are either obscene or child pornography.

Schools can disable the technology protection measures for adults' "*bona fide* research purposes," but they cannot disable the protections when minors are accessing the Internet, even with teacher or parental permission and supervision.

Technology Protection Measures
Under CIPA, a technology protection measure is narrowly defined as a specific technology that blocks or filters Internet access to the visual depictions discussed previously. Schools are not required to use electronic monitoring and data collection to monitor students' Internet use.

Surviving Constitutional Scrutiny
Although the American Civil Liberties Union and American Library Association-sponsored litigation challenging CIPA focuses on the act's requirements for libraries receiving federal technology funds, the litigation may also raise questions about CIPA's constitutionality when applied to schools. In May 2002, the Third District Court of Appeals ruled that CIPA impermissibly restricted the rights of adults to freely access the Internet in public libraries. Appeal of the decision will proceed directly to the U.S. Supreme Court. Even if the legal system proceeds with all possible haste, however, a decision regarding CIPA's applicability to library- and school-based Internet use is not likely until near the end of 2002. Meanwhile, schools must undertake action to comply with CIPA or risk losing e-rate funding. Over $2 billion in federal money is at stake.

APPENDIX C

A Suggested List of Policies and Standard Forms for School Districts

Policies

School districts, with the cooperation of their legal counsel and state and national school boards associations, should consider formulating and adopting the following policies pertaining to Internet accessibility and use in public schools. The list does not purport to be exhaustive or legally binding. School districts must take into account their unique circumstances, demographics, and community value systems when deciding what policies they need for the school Internet. Districts should include Internet policies in their school board policy manuals, their teacher contracts, and their student codes of conduct or disciplinary codes, when appropriate. With the exception of an Acceptable Use Policy (AUP), the following policies are only suggested, not required:

- An AUP on technology use by students and staff, including a statement of consequences resulting from the misuse of district technology equipment and services by students, teachers, administrators, and others having access to district facilities or resources.
- A policy listing mandatory technology competencies for students and current and prospective employees.

- A policy governing electronic publication of student- and employee-created works.
- A policy governing electronic publication of personally identifiable student information and photographs.
- A policy identifying the known and possible health risks of technology use.
- A policy on the use and distribution of copyrighted material on the Internet.
- A policy detailing what the district considers directory information.
- A policy stating parents' and community members' rights to access district Internet logs.
- A policy on Internet filtering and blocking of objectionable Internet content.
- A policy on parent and community involvement in Internet filtering and blocking decisions.
- A policy on assessing student technology fees.
- A policy requiring the approval of the district technology director or coordinator before creating, modifying, or uploading to district-affiliated Web sites.
- A policy requiring reporting of copyright violations on district-affiliated Web sites.
- A policy requiring reporting to the district technology director or coordinator of offensive Web sites that reference the district or district personnel.

Standard Forms

School districts can both ease the chores of teachers and other employees monitoring school Internet activities and encourage appropriate technology use by promulgating standard forms for reporting Internet permissions, activities, and abuses. A suggested, nonexhaustive list of possible standard district forms follows:

- A form for requesting permission to use copyrighted Internet material.

- A form for reporting copyright violations on district-sponsored or district-affiliated Web sites.
- A form for reporting offensive Web sites referencing the district or district personnel.
- A form for requesting permission to post student information, photographs, and original student work on the Internet.
- A form for requesting permission to post staff information, photographs, and original work on the Internet.
- A form for parents who wish to opt out of the district's posting of directory information about their child or family.
- A checklist for recording student progress toward achieving technology competencies.
- A checklist for recording staff progress toward achieving technology competencies.

General Resources

Researching Cases, Journal Articles, and Books about the Internet in Schools

Several Internet sites provide free, up-to-the-minute information about litigation and statutes, including summaries of pending cases and also actual court filings. Remember that the creator or sponsor of the Web site may select their content to reflect personal beliefs or advocate certain viewpoints. Read critically. The following two sites contain timely information:

- http://www.findlaw.com
- http://www.law.com

In addition to the Internet, several print publishers offer more in-depth information, including the following:

- West Publishers' *Education Law Reporter*. Published twice a month, the reporter contains the complete text of education-related cases decided in the U.S. Supreme Court, the Circuit Courts of Appeals, the U.S. District Courts, and State Appellate Courts. It also includes one or two scholarly, peer-reviewed articles per issue. The Reporter is generally available

only in law school libraries, but larger universities may have access via interlibrary loans.
- The *Journal of Law and Education*. This quarterly law journal also contains informative scholarly articles about the legal aspects of the Internet in schools.
- Finally, the National School Boards Association maintains a Web site listing a variety of books pertaining to technology in schools. The list is at http://www.nsba.org/itte/.

Professional Organizations as Sources of Information

Several professional organizations maintain Web sites that provide authoritative information on topics related to the Internet in schools and reprints of actual articles that appeared in their publications:

- The Association for Supervision and Curriculum Development Web site contains links to articles from its monthly magazine, *Educational Leadership*, at http://www.ascd.org.
- The Education Law Association maintains an informative Web site and articles from its publications at http://www.educationlaw.org.
- The National Education Association Web site is a general source of information about current issues of interest to school administrators and teachers. Their material is at http://www.nea.org.

Many state school board associations, like the National School Boards Association, maintain Web sites of particular interest not only to in-state school authorities, but also to out-of-state visitors. Use the "Search" function of your Internet browser to locate their Web sites.

Technology Standards

The complete sets of technology standards proposed for school administrators are available at the Web site of the International Society for Technology in Education, at http://www. iste.org.

Other Sources for Researching Case Law and Statutes

Online versions of newspapers are good sources of information. Many allow free searching of archives by topic or name. Most will at least allow searches for headlines or abstracts of stories, with fees required for access to full stories. For example, stories from the *New York Times* are available at http://www.nytimes.org. Online readers can even sign up for daily e-mail notification of stories selected from categories of interest. To follow developments in a specific case, accessing the local daily newspaper is often helpful. For example, to follow the *J.S. v. Bethlehem Area School District* litigation, access http://mcall.com, the Web site of the *Morning Call* newspaper in Allentown, Pennsylvania.

A technology newsletter available online, *eSchool News*, also provides an e-mail notification service. Their Web site is at http://www.eschoolnews.com.

Law School Web Sites

Law school Web sites are usually bias-free sources of legal information. The John Marshall Law School of Chicago, for example, maintains an extensive Web site at http://www.jmls.edu. Information on legal aspects of the Internet can be found at http://www.jmls.edu/cyber/index/index.html.

First Amendment Issues

- The American Civil Liberties Union (ACLU) maintains a very comprehensive Web site highlighting free speech issues at http://www.aclu.org.
- For privacy issues, checkout the Web site of the Electronic Privacy Institute at http://www.epic.org.
- The Center for Democracy & Technology also maintains an informative Web site at http://www.cdt.org.

Samples of School Internet Policies

One of the most comprehensive sources for samples and templates for such Internet-related school policies as Acceptable Use Policies (AUPs), privacy policies, and Internet policies in general is the Web site maintained by the Virginia Department of Education's Department of Technology. Besides providing helpful general information, Virginia's Web site embeds links to other sites maintained by different state departments of education and professional organizations and societies. The Virginia Department of Education home page can be found at http://www.pen. k12.va.us.

About the Author

KATHLEEN CONN IS AN EDUCATOR AND PUBLIC SCHOOL ADMINISTRATOR as well as a lawyer and member of the Pennsylvania Bar. Conn earned her Ph.D. in Physics/Biology at Bryn Mawr College, studying molecular dynamics with pulsed nuclear magnetic resonance techniques. She completed postdoctoral work in the cell biology of cancer metastasis at Lankenau Medical Research Center in Philadelphia. She has taught science and problem solving at the secondary, college, and graduate levels, both in the United States and abroad. Conn also has been a delegate to international conferences on physics education and a member of the Advisory Council for both the Mechanical Universe High School Adaptation (MUHSA) and the Comprehensive Conceptual Curriculum for Physics (C3P), two National Science Foundation (NSF)-sponsored exemplary pre-college physics curriculum projects.

Conn returned to student status to earn her J.D. degree at Widener University School of Law, Evening Division, while making the transition to public school administration. For the past six years, she has been a K–12 curriculum supervisor in the West Chester Area School District.

Conn is the author of numerous journal articles in the areas of science research, science education, and education law. She is a frequent presenter at local and national conferences of the National Science Teachers' Association, Technology Education Association, and the Education Law Association, and consults on issues of safety in the science classroom, teacher liability, and Internet issues in public schools. She has also presented papers at science and education conferences in Canada and Europe.